2-D Nano Materials and their Hybrids as Supercapacitor Electrodes for Energy Storage Applications

Shibsankar Dutta

2D nano materials and their hybrids as supercapacitor electrodes
for energy storage applications

First Edition October 2024

Written by Shibsankar Dutta

Table of Contents

Chapter 1. Introduction   1-6

1.1 . Motivation

1.2 . Aim and Objective

1.3 . Novelty

1.4 . Thesis structure

1.5 . References

Chapter 2. Literature Review   7-34

2.1 History of supercapacitor

2.2 Specific energy and specific power comparison of ECSs, batteries and fuel cells

2.3 Classification of Supercapacitors

    2.3.1 Electric double layer mechanism

    2.3.2 Pseudo-capacitance mechanism

2.4 Supercapacitor material selection

    2.4.1 Electrode materials for Supercapacitor

    2.4.1.1. Zero dimensional materials (0-D)

        2.4.1.1.a. Solid 0-D nanostructures

        2.4.1.1.b. Hollow 0-D nanostructures

        2.4.1.1.c. Core–shell 0D nanostructures

    2.4.1.2. One dimensional materials (1-D)

        2.4.1.2.a 1-D Homostructures

        2.4.1.2.b 1-D Heterostructures

    2.4.1.3. Two dimensional materials (2-D)

        2.4.1.3.a 2-D Homostructures

            2.4.1.3.a (i)Graphene

            2.4.1.3.a (ii) Metal oxides and hydroxides

            2.4.1.3.a (iii) Transition metal dichalcogenides (TMDs)

            2.4.1.3.a (iv)Transition metal carbides and/or nitrides(MXenes)

        2.4.1.3.b 2-D Homostructures

Chapter 3. Measurement and Characterization Tools 35-46

Chapter 7. MoS$_2$ Nanosheets/rGO Hybrid: An Electrode Material for High Performance Thin Film Supercapacitor

Chapter 8. Vanadyl Phosphate Nano sheets-MWCNT Composite Free standing thin film For Supercapacitor Application

List of Abbreviations

0D, 1D, 2D, 3D   Zero, One, Two, Three Dimensional

A

AFM   Atomic Force Microscope

B

$BiVO_4$ Bismuth vanadate

BiOCl   Bismuth oxychloride

C

CV   Cyclic voltammetry

CNTs   Carbon nanotubes

CMG   Chemically modified graphene

Co_3O_4 Cobalt oxide

D

DMSO   Dimethyl sulfoxide

DMF   Dimethylformamide

E

EDLC   Electric double layer capacitor

ESPW   Electrochemical stable potential window

ESR   Equivalent series resistance

EDX   Energy dispersive X-ray

EIS   Electrochemical impedance spectroscopy

ECS   Electrochemical supercapacitor

F

FESEM   Field emission scanning electron microscope

Fe_3O_4, Fe_2O_3 Iron Oxide

FSSSC   Flexible solid state symmetric supercapacitor

G

GA   Graphene analogue

GO   Graphene oxide

GCD   Galvanometric charging discharging

H

HRTEM   High-resolution Transmission Electron Microscope

HSP   Hansen solubility parameter

HSCs   Hybrid supercapacitors

H_2SO_4 Sulphuric acid

I

IHP   Inner Helmholtz plane

IrO_2 Iridium (IV) oxide

K

KCl   Potassium Chloride

KI   Potassium Iodide

KOH   Potassium hydroxide

L

LIB   Lithium ion battery

M

MoO_3 — Molybdenum Trioxide

MnO_2 — Manganese (IV) Oxide

MWCNT nanotube — Multiwall Carbon

MXenes and/or nitrides — Transition metal carbides

N

Na_2SO_4 — Sodium sulfate

NiO — Nickel oxide

NMP — N-Methyl-2-pyrrolidone

NaOH — Sodium Hydroxide

O

OHP — Outer Helmholtz plane

P

PET — Polyethylene Terephthalate

PSCs — Pseudo supercapacitor

PVA — Polyvinyl Alcohol

PVP — Polyvinylpyrrolidone

PEO — Polyethylene glycol

PAA — Polypolyacrylate

PVDF — Polyvinylidene fluoride

PEDOT: PSS — Poly(3,4-Ethylenedioxythiophene):Poly(Styrene-Sulfonate)

R

rGO — Reduced graphene oxide

RuO_2 — Ruthenium (IV) Oxide

R_{ct} — Charge transfer resistance

S

SWCNT nanotube — Single wall carbon

SCs — Supercapacitors

SDS — Sodium dodecylsulphate

SNAP — Spin-on nano imprinting

T

TMOs — Transition metal oxides

TMDCs — Transition metal dichalcogenides

U

UV-Vis-NIR — Ultraviolet-visible-near infrared spectrophotometer

V

VS_2 — Vanadium disulfide

$VOPO_4$ — Vanadium phosphate

V_2O_5 — Vanadium pent oxide

W

WS_2 — Tungsten disulfide

X

XPS — X-ray photoelectron spectroscopy

XRD — X-Ray Diffractometer

List of Figures

Chapter 2

Chapter 3

Chapter 4

Chapter 5

Chapter 7

Chapter 8

List of Tables

Chapter 1

Introduction

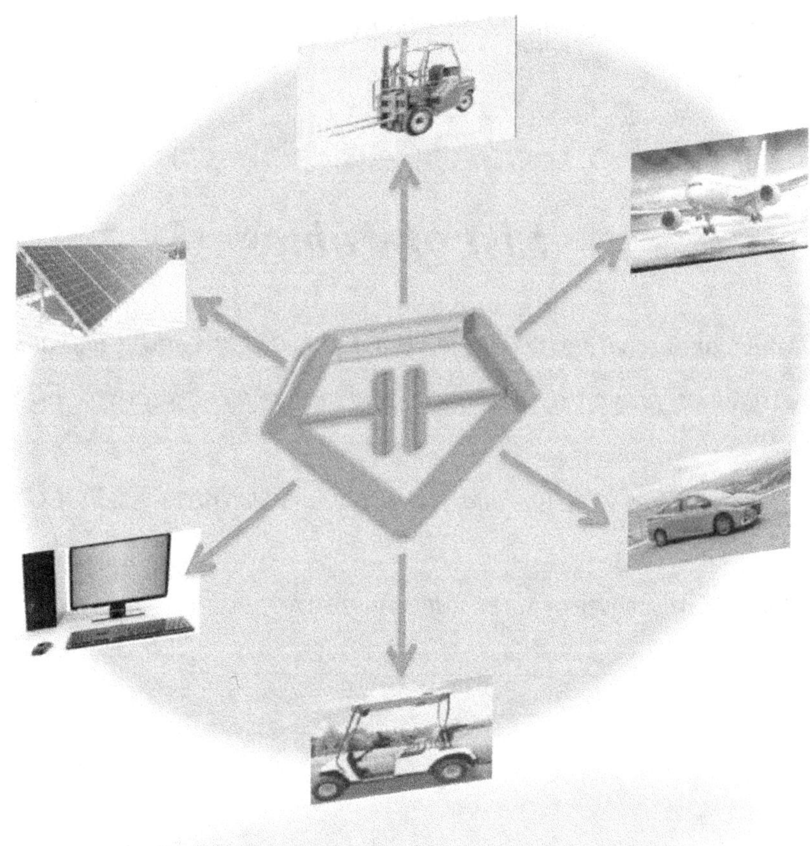

1. Introduction

Electrochemical capacitors or Supercapacitors is an electrochemical energy storage device which converts electrochemical energy in to the electrical energy. Two electrode supercapacitor consist two high specific surface area based electrodes, situated both sides of a separator that contain the electrolyte whereas in three electrode supercapacitor active material, Ag/AgCl or $Hg/HgCl_2$ and platinum wire are acts as working electrode, reference and counter electrode respectively.[1] Depending on the charge storage mechanisms supercapacitors can be classified into three types.[2] Most common type of SCs are electrochemical double layer capacitor (EDLC), which can store energy using ion adsorption and use carbon based active material like Graphene ,carbon nanotubes.[3-7] In transition metal oxides (TMOs),[8-16] transition metal dichalcogenides (TMDCs),[17] hydroxides[18-20] and conductive polymer[21-24] based supercapacitor energy is stored due to fast and reversible surface redox reaction occurring at the surface of the active electrode materials, which are known as pseudocapacitor (PSCs). Advanced approaches to increase the specific capacitance and energy density are to develop hybrid electrode materials for supercapacitor by adding electrochemically active materials with carbonaceous materials. This kind of SCs knows as Hybrid supercapacitors (HSCs).

1.1 Motivation

Now a day, it is next to impossible to imagine our lives without wearable and portable electronic devices such as smartphones, laptops, e-papers, cameras, displays, transplantable medical devices, smart watch and many more, which play an effective role to change new generation's life style. With the decreasing availability of fossil fuel, increasing pollution associated with their use and ever growing demand of energy consumption of these kinds of smart electronics requires superior energy storage devices. According to Ragone chessboard, though supercapacitors (SCs) and batteries are the most successful players but due to the higher power density, cycle efficiency and charging-discharging rate supercapacitors play leading role over other energy storage devices like lithium ion battery (LIB).[1] Yet, a number of nano structured pseudocapacitive electrode materials such as nano particles, nanorods, nanospheres, nanosheets etc. have attracted for supercapacitor applications. Among them two dimensional (2-D) graphene analogues (GA) are the best for the highly flexible ultrathin-film supercapacitor in all-solid-state with higher energy density and excellent mechanical flexibility.[17,18,25]Two-dimensional (2-D) nanomaterials offer exciting prospects for both fundamental studies and several technological applications due to their unique and intriguing properties.[26-30] Materials with intrinsic layered structure provide scope for the production of 2-D systems with a very broad range of properties. In their 2-D structure, inorganic layered materials such as transition metal oxides (MnO_2, RuO_2, MoO_3, TiO_2 etc.) and transition metal dichalcogenides (MoS_2, WS_2, VS_2, etc.) for their unique properties becomes promising candidates for topological insulators, energy harvesters, thermal conductors, and transistors. [31-36]

1.2 Objective

The main focus of this dissertation is to get a better understanding about the electrochemical behaviour of the 2-D nano materials to fabricate of hybrid SCs with the carbonaceous electrode materials using aqueous and solid (gel electrolyte) electrolytes for two electrode and three electrode supercapacitor applications.

The objectives of this thesis are:

1. Large scale production of 2-D nano materials by facial low cost environmental friendly mixed solvent exfoliation, hydrothermal or solvothermal process.
2. Fabrication of hybrids or composite flexible supercapacitors based on 2-D nano materials with high energy density.
3. High performance of supercapacitor with excellent cycle stability.

1.3 Novelty

Present work reported large scale production of 2-D materials using mixed solvent exfoliation from their bulk forms and Hydro (or solvo) thermally synthesized layered materials also exfoliated by liquid phase exfoliation by suitable solvents. These well dispersed stable solutions were used to make thin films which can be readily transferred on wide range of substrates for flexible supercapacitor electrode applications with high energy density. The performance of the composite electrode materials by varying compositions also included in the present work. The specific novelty claims in this thesis are listed below

- Mixed solvent exfoliation of 2-D nano materials.
- Few layered 2-D materials and their hybrids or composites with graphene and CNTs thin films on different substrates for flexible supercapacitor application

> ➢ An investigation the performance of 2-D materials based solid state supercapacitor varying compositions and optimised the best composition endowed with high energy density.

1.4 Thesis structure

The chapter1 contains the introduction of this research. The literature review of electrochemical capacitors is given in the chapter 2, containing a picture of the growth of supercapacitors from conventional capacitors, selection of electrode materials, electrolytes and synthesis of 2-D nano materials respectively. The chapter3 presents different measurement and characterization tools and the electrochemical performance measurement techniques for supercapacitors. Chapter 4 provides a novel mixed solvent exfoliation process to prepare transition metal oxide nanosheets for thin film flexible supercapacitor application. The chapter5 presents $BiVO_4$/rGO hybrid electrode material with optimised weight percentage of $BiVO_4$ for superior electrochemical performance. The chapter6 provides highly crystalline 2-D BiOCl nanoplate and their composites with MWCNT for flexible supercapacitor with excellent cycle stability. We have reported we have used SWCNT network as a current collector instead of gold which will be helpful to make transparent flexible supercapacitor. The chapter7 presents large scale production of MoS_2 and MoS_2/rGO hybrid by simple hydrothermal route followed by liquid phase exfoliation to get the nanosheets. These MoS_2 nanosheets in presence of rGO exhibit excellent electrochemical performances. The chapter 8 contains $VOPO_4$ and MWCNT composite electrode material fabrication and the electrochemical. The chapter 9 provides overall conclusions and future work.

1.5 References

1. H. Wang, H. S. Casalongue, Y. Liang and H. Dai, *J. Am.Chem. Soc.* 2010, **132**, 7472–7477.

2. M. Winter and R. J. Brodd, *Chem. Rev.* 2004, **104**, 4245– 4270.

3. J. Huang, B. G. Sumpter and V. Meunier, Angew. Chem., Int. Ed., 2008, **47**, 520–524

4. J. Gamby, P. Taberna, P. Simon, J. Fauvarque and M. Chesneau, *J. Power Sources* 2001, **101**, 109–116.

5. D. N. Futaba, K. Hata, T. Yamada, T. Hiraoka, Y. Hayamizu,Y. Kakudate, O. Tanaike, H. Hatori, M. Yumura and S. Iijima, *Nat. Mater.* 2006, **5**, 987–994.

6.   Y. Wang, Z. Shi, Y. Huang, Y. Ma, C. Wang, M. Chen and Y. Chen, *J. Phys. Chem. C* 2009, **113**, 13103–13107.

7.   L. L. Zhang, R. Zhou and X. Zhao, *J. Mater. Chem.* 2010, **20**, 5983–5992.

8.   W. Tang, L. Liu, S. Tian, L. Li, Y. Yue, Y. Wu and K. Zhu, *Chem. Commun.* 2011 **47**, 10058-10060.

9.   F. Luan, G. Wang, Y. Ling, X. Lu, H. Wang, Y. Tong, X.X. Liu and Y. Li, *Nanoscale* 2013, **5**, 7984-7990.

10.   C.C. Hu, K.H. Chang, M.C. Lin and Y.T. Wu, *Nano Lett.* 2006, **6**, 2690-2695.

11.   X. Lu, G. Wang, T. Zhai, M. Yu, J. Gan, Y. Tong and Y. Li, *Nano Lett.* 2012, **12**, 1690-1696.

12.   X. Lu, T. Zhai, X. Zhang, Y. Shen, L. Yuan, B. Hu, L. Gong, J. Chen, Y. Gao, J. Zhou, Y. Tong and Z. L. Wang, *Adv. Mater.* 2012, **24**, 938-944.

13.   G. Yu, L. Hu, N. Liu, H. Wang, M. Vosgueritchian, Y. Yang, Y. Cui and Z. Bao, *Nano Lett.*2011, **11**, 4438-4442.

14.   G. Yu, L. Hu, M. Vosgueritchian, H. Wang, X. Xie, J. R. McDonough, X. Cui, Y. Cui and Z. Bao, *Nano Lett.* 2011, **11**, 2905-2911.

15.   L. Wu, R. Li, J. Guo, C. Zhou, W. Zhang, C. Wang, Y. Huang, Y. Li and J. Liu, *AIP Adv.*2013, **3**, 082129.

16.   L. Peng, X. Peng, B. Liu, C. Wu, Y. Xie and G. Yu, *Nano Lett.*2013, **13**, 2151-2157.

17.   J. Feng, X. Sun, C. Wu, L. Peng, C. Lin, S. Hu, J. Yang and Y. Xie, *J. Am. Chem. Soc.* 2011, **133**, 17832-17838.

18.   J. Xie, X. Sun, N. Zhang, K. Xu, M. Zhou and Y. Xie, *Nano Energy* 2013, **2**, 65-74.

19.   J. Yan, Z. Fan, W. Sun, G. Ning, T. Wei, Q. Zhang, R. Zhang, L. Zhi and F. Wei, *Adv. Funct. Mater.*2012, **22**, 2632-2641.

20.   V. Gupta, T. Kusahara, H. Toyama, S. Gupta and N. Miura, *Electrochem. Commun.* 2012, **9**, 2315-2319.

21.   H. Wang, Q. Hao, X. Yang, L. Lu and X. Wang, *Nanoscale* 2010, **2**, 2164-2170.

22.   K. Jurewicz, S. Delpeux, V. Bertagna, F. Beguin and E. Frackowiak, *Chem. Phys. Lett.* 2001, **347**, 36-40.

23.   J. Tao, N. Liu, W. Ma, L. Ding, L. Li, J. Su and Y. Gao, *Sci. Rep.* 2013, **3**, 2286.

24.   A. Laforgue, P. Simon, C. Sarrazin, J. F. Fauvarque, *J. Power Sources* 1999, **80**, 142-148.

25. J. J. Yoo, K. Balakrishnan, J. Huang, V. Meunier, B. G. Sumpter, A. Srivastava, M. Conway, A. L. M. Reddy, J. Yu, R. Vajtai and P. M. Ajayan, *Nano Lett.* 2011, **11**, 1423-1427.

26. X. Huang, X. Qi, F. Boey and H. Zhang, *Chem. Soc. Rev.* 2012, **41**, 666-686.

27. A. K. Geim and K. S. Novoselov, *Nat. Mater.* 2007, **6**, 183-191.

28. X. Huang, C.Tan, Z. Yin, and H. Zhang, *Adv. Mater.* 2014, **26**, 2185-2204.

29. F. Bonaccorso, L. Colombo, G. Yu, M. Stoller, V. Tozzini, A. C. Ferrari, R. S. Ruoff, V. Pellegrini. *Science* 2015, **41**, 347.

30. S. Dutta, S. Pal, and S. De, *New J. Chem.* 2018, **42**, 10161-10166.

31. G. Wang, X.G. Zhu, Y.Y. Sun, Y.Y. Li, T. Zhang, J. Wen, X.Chen, K. He, L.L. Wang, X.C. Ma, J.F. Jia, S. B. Zhang and Q.K. Xue,. *Adv. Mater.* 2011, **23**, 2929-2932.

32. C. Y. Zhi, Y. Bando, C. C. Tang, H. Kuwahara, D. Golberg, *Adv. Mater.* 2009, **21**, 2889-2893.

33. B. Radisavljevic, A. Radenovic, J. Brivio, V. Giacometti, A. Kis, *Nat. Nanotechnol.* 2011, **6**, 147-150.

34. W. J. Yu, S. Y. Lee, S. H. Chae, D. Perello, G. H. Han, M. Yun and Y. H. Lee, *Nano Lett.* 2011, **11**, 1344-1350.

35. S. Yin, Y. Zhang, J. Kong, C. Zou, C. M. Li, X. Lu, J. Ma, F. Y. C. Boey, X. Chen, *ACS Nano.* 2011, **5**, 3831-3838.

36. K.Chang, and W.Chen,.*ACS Nano.* 2011, **5**, 4720-4728.

Chapter 2

Literature review

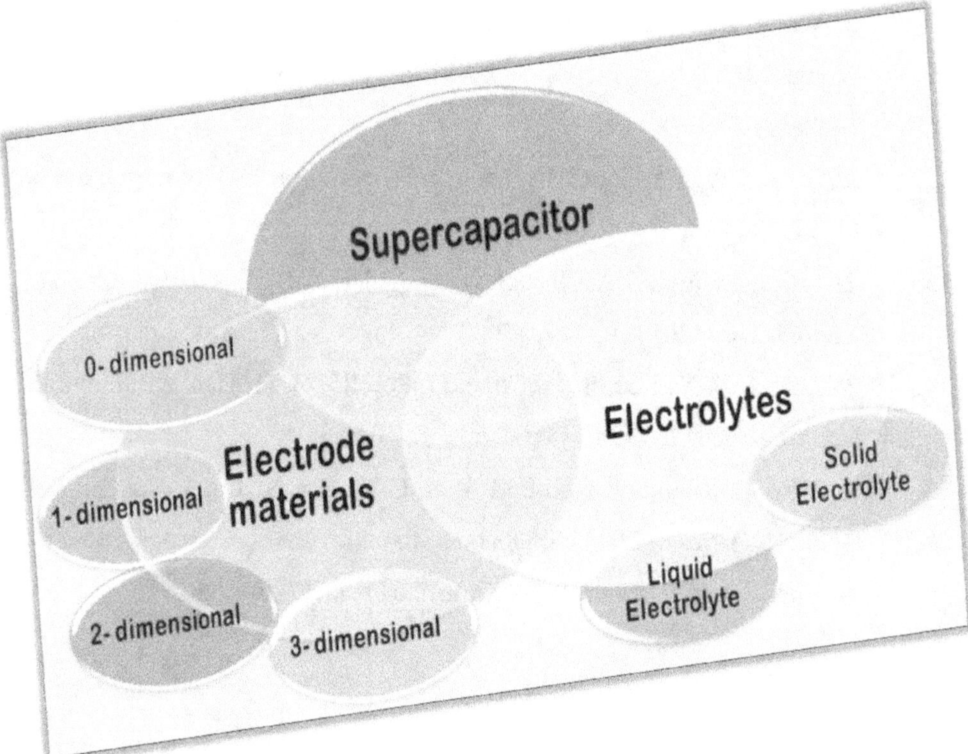

2. Literature review

2.1 History of supercapacitor

Capacitors are well known passive circuit elements, which can store electrical energy temporarily. The charge storage phenomena was first observed by Ewald Georg von Kleist of Pomerania, in a water filled hand held glass jar in the year of 1745. In 1746, Pieter van Musschenbroek, a Dutch physicist discovered a similar kind of capacitor known as Leyden jar. In the following year the Daniel Gralath improved the performance of Leyden jar by combine several jars. The improved flat capacitor design as show in the fig2.1 (a) was then proposed by Benjamin Franklin. The electrolytic capacitors having same anode and cathode materials with cell structure like batteries was the next step in the growth of capacitor devices. Before invention of supercapacitor, aluminium ceramic capacitors were the mostly used electrolytic capacitors. In aluminium electrolytic capacitors, among the two pieces of aluminium foil one was etched to form aluminium oxide's thin layer which acts as dielectric as shown the cross sectional view of the device fig 2.1 (b).

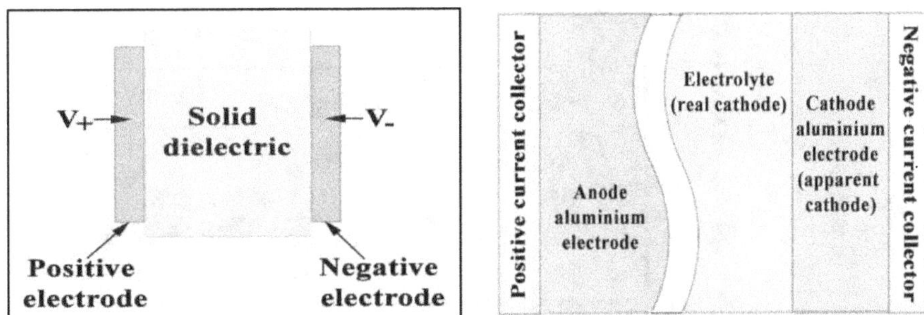

Figure.2.1 Schematic of (a) Electrostatic capacitor, (b) Aluminium electrolytic capacitors.

The electric double layer capacitor was the third generation evolution of capacitive devices. The first electric double layer capacitor was discovered in 1957 by general electric engineers, where they used porous carbon and aqueous electrolyte. At the initial stage, it was believed that energy was stored in the pores of the porous carbon although the mechanism was unknown at that time. Later, Standard Oil of Ohio's **(SOHIO)** used activated charcoal as electrode materials and an insulating thin separator in between to develop a new design of electrochemical capacitor, which serves as the basis design of the supercapacitor to date. They failed to commercialize it and sold the technology to

NEC which then commercialized in 1978. Tassati and Buzanca examined the performance of ruthenium oxides in the year of 1971 and observed the same electrochemical behaviour with a capacitor.[1,2] Further, more research was carried out on the supercapacitor based on ruthenium oxide in between 1975 to 1980. Initially after its discovery, it was mainly used as a power backup in the computers and from mid-90's to date some companies such as Panasonic, NEC/TOKIN, Maxwell Technologies others invest for the development of electrochemical capacitors. From the market analysis done by Lux Research, it was observed that, the market for ECS was estimated to about $208 million in 2009 while in 2014 it reached $877 million and continues to increase in the resent years due to its application in cell phones, digital cameras and smart grid etc.[3-5]

2.2 Specific energy and specific power comparison of ECSs, batteries and fuel cells

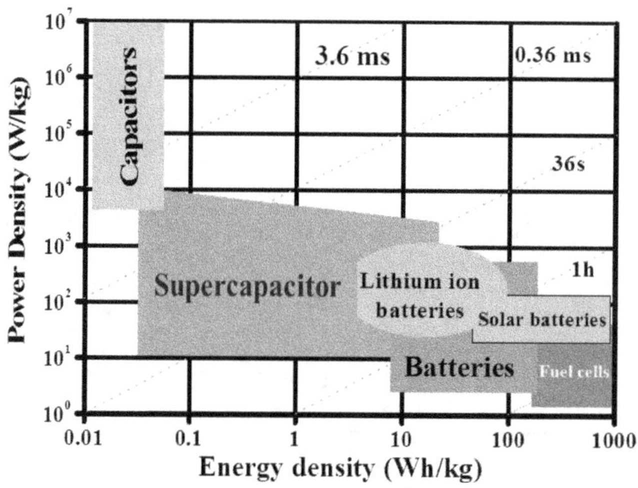

Figure 2.2 Ragone plots of different energy storage devices.

The energy storage performance of different energy storage systems can be characterised by Ragone plot as shown in the fig 2.2. The require time for charging and discharging of the various energy storage systems are represented by the dash lines. From the Ragone plot it is visualise that capacitors have greater specific power compare to fuel cells and batteries but its energy density is much lower compare to the fuel cells and batteries, which indicates that charging discharging of capacitors is very fast and produces high power but it can store low energy per unit mass or volume, whereas batteries take large time for charging and discharging but high specific energy storage property. Supercapacitor fills the power gap between capacitors and batteries since supercapacitor have greater power density than batteries and high energy density than conventional capacitors.

2.3 Classification of Supercapacitors

Supercapacitors can be classified into three types based on their charge storage mechanism known as electrical double-layer capacitors (EDLCs), pseudocapacitors (PSCs) and hybrid capacitors(HSCs) as shown in the fig2.3.[6] Carbon based (such as active material like Graphene, carbon aerogel, carbon nanotubes etc.) EDLC is most common used supercapacitor.[6,7-10] The transition metal oxides (ruthenium oxide, manganese oxide, tin oxide, cobalt oxide)[11-19] transition metal dichalcogenides (TMDCs),[20] hydroxides [21-23] and conductive polymer (polyaniline, polypyrrole, polythiophene). [24-27] are most commonly used electrode materials for pseudocapacitor. Low capacitance in EDLC and poor cycle's stability in pseudocapacitors confines their practical application. Innovative approaches to raise the specific capacitance, stability and energy density are to develop hybrid electrode materials for supercapacitor by adding electrochemically active materials with carbonaceous materials. This kind of SCs knows as Hybrid supercapacitors (HSCs).

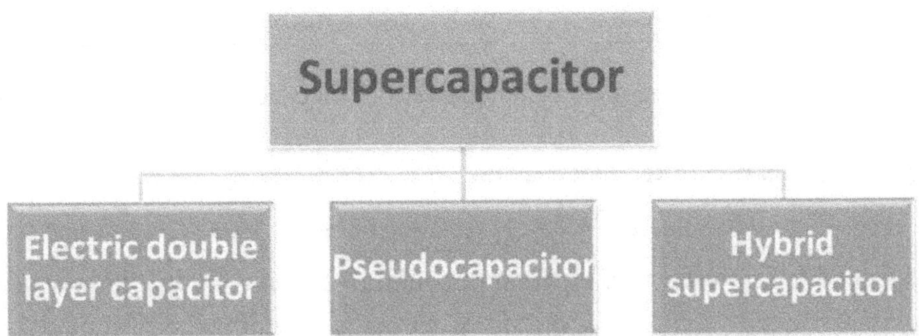

Figure2.3 Schematic of Classification of Supercapacitor

2.3.1 Electric double layer mechanism

In the 19th century, von Helmholtz was first described the idea of double layers, which consist of few nanometres thick double layers of opposite charge forms between the electrode/electrolyte interface(Figure 2.4a), where energy stored due to ion adsorption. Further it was understood that ions on the electrolyte side of the double layer suffered thermal fluctuation according to the Boltzmann principle, as a result of that ions could not remain static in the form of compact array. Later, Gouy and Chapman improved the Helmholtz double-layer model. According to the Gouy–Chapman a diffuse layer is formed due to the thermal fluctuation of the electrolyte ions as shown in the figure 2.4(b). In the Gouy–Chapman model ions were considered as point charges. Combining Helmholtz model with Gouy–Chapman model, Stern presented a model, which describe compact and diffusion region explicitly. The compact layer made of by inner Helmholtz plane (IHP), which is the distance of closest approach of adsorbed ions and outer Helmholtz plane (OHP) refers the plane where the diffusion layer start. According to the Stern model capacitance of the EDLC is the series combination of stern layer capacitance and diffusion layer capacitance as shown in the figure 2.4(c).

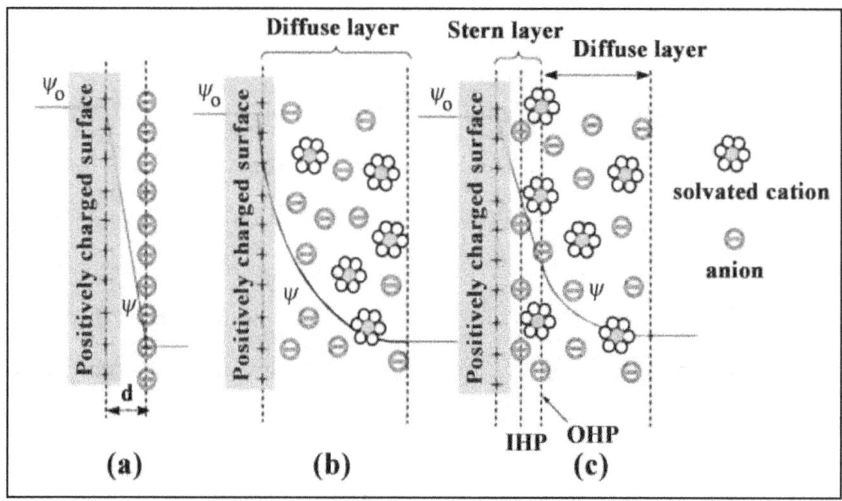

Figure2.4 Schematic of mechanism of electric double layer capacitor.

2.3.2 Pseudocapacitance mechanism

In case of pseudocapacitor a fast reversible Faradaic (redox) reactions takes place on the electrode in presence of external potential. B.E. Conway in 1970 was fast discussed there are mainly three faradic mechanisms process involves in pseudocapacitive behaviour: (1) under potential deposition, (2) redox pseudocapacitance and (3) intercalation pseudocapacitance as shown in the fig 2.5. Langmuir type electroporation of H on the noble metal substrate is an example of under potential deposition, where adsorbed monolayer of the metal ions obtain on the different metal substrate at well above their redox potential. The ions are electrochemically adsorbed onto active material's surface in case of redox pseudocapacitance, whereas ion intercalation into sheets of an active material without any crystallographic phase change terms as intercalation pseudocapacitance.

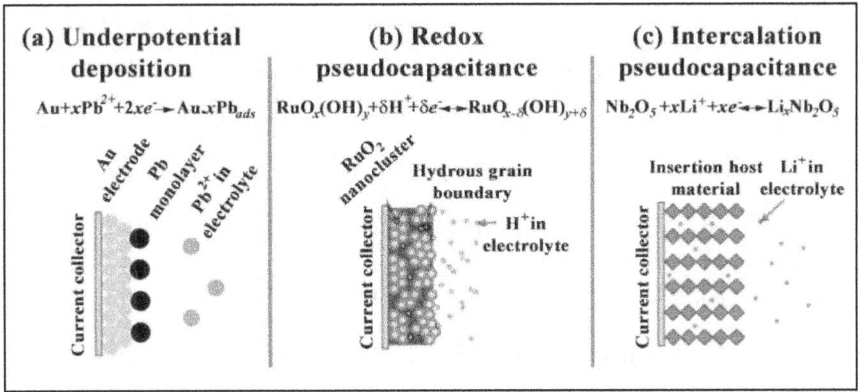

Figure2.5 Schematic of mechanism of pseudocapacitors

2.4 Supercapacitor material selection

Energy density of the supercapacitor is directly proportional to the square of the voltage window as well as the capacitance value, so enhancement of the energy density can be done by increasing both voltage window and capacitance value. Notably, the electrode material's structure and morphology and electrolyte's composition is closely linked with both of voltage window as well as capacitance.

2.4.1 Electrode materials for Supercapacitor

Specific capacitance, energy density, power density and stability are the key performance parameters of supercapacitors and these parameters are directly depends on the electrode materials. An ideal electrode material should have the following properties:

- High specific surface area.
- Extra electroactive sites.
- Porous structure.
- High electronic conductivity.
- High thermal and chemical stability.
- Low cost of raw materials.

Nanostructures of the electrode materials also play an importance role to achieve the aforementioned factors. Different nanostructures material can be categorised into zero dimension (0-D), one dimensional (1-D), two dimensional (2-D) and three dimension (3-D) respectively.[28] Spherical or nearly spherical nanoparticles with an aspect ratio close to 1 are fall under the 0-D category and quantum dots, nanoparticles, nanosphere etc. are belongs from these category. Fiber like shaped nanomaterial with high aspect ratio such as nanotubes, nanowires, nanofibers, nanopillars, nanobelts etc. are considered as 1-D. One or few atomic layer nanomaterial's with higher bond strength than three dimensions are defined as two dimensional (2-D) nanomaterial. They include Graphene, Graphene oxides, and other layered materials such as MoS_2, VS_2, MoO_3, $VOPO_4$ etc. Carbon nanofoams, 3-D porous carbon and Graphene aerogel are regarded as three dimensional (3-D) electrode materials for supercapacitors.

2.4.1.1 Zero dimensional nanomaterials (0-D)

Nanomaterials with three dimensions constrained on nanoscale are defined as 0-D nanomaterials which have three subclasses solid zero dimensional, hollow zero dimensional and core-shell zero dimensional nanostructures. In this type of materials electrons are confined in all three directions.

2.4.1.1.a. Solid 0-D nanostructures

Among different nanostructures, solid 0-D nanostructures such as ACs, carbon nanospheres, transition metal oxides (e.g. RuO_2[29], NiO[30, 31, 32] Fe_3O_4[33], MnO_2[34]) are generally used as electrode materials for supercapacitor. Chemically or physically synthesized activated carbon from various carbonaceous precursors like coal, wood etc. are one of the most commonly used carbon based materials in supercapacitor because ACs provides greater specific surface area even up to 3000 m^2/g.[35] Though ACs have high surface area, the obtained specific capacitance of ACs based supercapacitors are quiet small ($<10\mu F/cm^2$), because specific capacitance is also depends on the distributions of pore sizes , electronic conductivity and electrolyte's accessibility too. Gogotsi, Simon et.al reported carbon onion having surface area 500 m^2/g showed better electrochemical performance that ACs. This is due the fact that for onion like structure, surface is fully oven to the electrolyte ions.[36,37] The above mention criteria are also applicable for pseudocapacitive materials such as TMOs, TMDCs etc. Conducting nano porous gold/MnO_2 hybrid exhibited specific capacitance of 1145 F/g at 50mV/s, because nano porous gold provides an easy path to access the electrons and ions.[38] K. J. Stevenson and co-worker reported, $LaMnO_3$ nanoparticles based supercapacitor, which obtained 610 F/g capacitance at scan rate of 2 mV/s. For perovskite-type materials also store charge through oxygen intercalation.[39] Hence, besides the activated carbon and TMOs, perovskite materials are the new candidate for supercapacitor applications.

2.4.1.1.b. Hollow 0-D nanostructures

The properties like short transportation path of charge, low density and high surface to volume ratio of hollow 0-D materials make them attractive candidates for supercapacitor application. For the synthesis of hollow 0-D materials, there are three different procedures such as template-free, soft templating and hard templating. The controlled shape, size and structure of 0-D nanomaterials can easily achieved by hard templating methods rather than the other two as mention above. Hollow carbon nanosphere obtained by hard templating method delivered large specific surface area up to 1704 m^2/g and 1.6 cm^3/g pore volume with ~6.4 nm pore width. The hollow carbon nano sphere based supercapacitor exhibits 251 F/g specific capacitance value at 50 mV/s scan rate.[40] Furthermore, multiple shelled hollow 0-D structure of the nano materials such as Fe_2O_3, MnO_2, NiO, and Co_3O_4 has been studied as well.[41-47] Zhang et.al was reported Single, double, and triple shelled NiO nanospheres. Among them double layer NiO nanospheres exhibits 92.00 m^2/g surface area with 612.5 F/g specific capacitance.[48]

2.4.1.1.c. Core–shell 0D nanostructures

The thin shell coated hollow or solid nano particle is known as core-shell 0-D nano structure. A core-shell nano structure prepared by combining carbonises and faradic materials show good mechanical and chemical stability, least agglomeration and improved electrical conductivity.[49-51] Zhao et.al reported hollow carbon sphere/polyaniline (PANI) core-shell structure exhibits 525 F/g specific capacitance, whereas that for hollow carbon sphere is only 268 F/g.[52] With increasing amount of PANI, electrochemical performance of the electrode materials becomes poor; this is due to the fact that with increasing PANI pores will be blocked and reduced accessibility of ions. Zhao and co-worker have grown MnO_2 shell on carbon core as supercapacitor electrode materials by direct redox reaction at 70°C using hollow spheres of graphitic carbon and potassium permanganate solution. The hybrid core-shell structures with 64 wt% MnO_2 displayed 190 F/g specific capacitance at 0.1 A/ g.[50]

2.4.1.2 One dimensional nanomaterials (1-D)

Fiber shaped nanomaterials with high aspect ratio is categorised as 1-D nano-structures. Nanotube, nano fibres, nano wire, nano pillar, nano rods etc. fall into that category.1-D nano-structures have good chemical and physical properties. 1-D nano-structures also provide decent electrical transport properties to increase the kinetics of the electrochemical reactions. Due to the above mentioned properties 1-D nano-structures have been widely examined for the electrode materials for supercapacitors. Homostructures and heterostructures are two main categories of 1D nanostructure.

2.4.1.2.a 1-D Homostructures

1-D homostructures can be define as a structure which contain only one particular structure like nanorods, nanotubes, nanofibers etc. 1-D homostructures can be classified into three groups such as nanotubes, nanorods/nanopillars and nanowires.

Nanorods/nanopillars having aspect ratios less than 10, which confines the improvement of surface area of the nanorods compared to nanowires. Thomas and co-workers have synthesized highly ordered carbon nanopillars of diameter and length 95 nm and 200 nm respectively prepared by simple, rapid and cost-effective spin-on nano imprinting technique. The highly ordered carbon nanopillars electrode exhibits specific capacitance of $3.4mF/cm^2$.[53] Tong et.al reported oxygen deficient Fe_2O_3 nanorods based supercapacitor, which obtained 64.5 F/g specific capacitance.[54]

High aspect ratio (>10) of nanowires not only enhance the charge transportation path also offer large surface area on to which charges are stored, and due to that reason we get enriched electrochemical performance. The vertically aligned PANI nanowires based electrochemical capacitor showed 1142 F/g specific capacitance at a current density of 5 A/g.[55] Horng and co-workers have successfully synthesized PANI nanowires on Carbon cloth, which delivered highest specific capacitance of 1079 F/g, at 1.73 A/g with 86% capacitive retention after 2100 cycles.[56] Recently, ternary metallic oxides have attracted significant attention as electrode materials due to their multiple oxide states. Lou et.al reported $NiCo_2O_4$ nanoneedle electrode supercapacitor showed 1118.6 F/g specific capacitance.[57] Nanotubes offer greater specific surface area per unit mass than solid nanowires or nanofibers because of their hollow interior structure. As a result specific capacitance also enhanced with compare to the solid 1-D nano structures. Xai and co-worker have compared the performance of MnO_2 nanotube and MnO_2 nanowire as electrode material.[58] The MnO_2 nanotube and MnO_2 nanowire obtained a specific capacitance of 320 F/g, and 101 F/g respectively. Chi Chang Hu and co-worker have successfully synthesized RuO_2 nanotube array by deposition technique which exhibited 550 F/g specific capacitance.[59] Carbon nano tubes are one of the most used 1-D nano materials for supercapacitor electrode application because its provides high electronic conductivity, decent thermal and mechanical stability, high specific surface area and porosity. H. Pan and his group reported pure CNT based electrode obtained highest specific capacitance of 100 F/g.[60]

2.4.1.2.b 1-D Heterostructures

Recently, 1-D heterostructures having more than one component considered as one of the probable candidates for supercapacitor electrode because synergic enhancement of properties such as electrical conductivity, ionic transport, mechanical stability and electrochemical reversibility after heterostructures formation. 1-D core-shell heterostructures provides enhanced cycles stability and better electrochemical performance than other heterostructures due their exclusive structural properties that reduced the aggregation chance of the active materials as well as overcome the side reaction problem between active materials and electrolyte. P.L.Taberna et.al reported Cu/Fe_3O_4 core shell nanostructure. There are several core shell nanostructure such as Au/MnO_2, Ni/MnO_2, Ni/Co_3O_4, Mn/MnO_2, $AuPd/MnO_2$, $CuO/AuPd/MnO_2$, Ni/NiO have been already reported as supercapacitor electrodes.[28] Zhai and co-workers reported $CNT/PPy–MnO_2$ core shell nano structure based supercapacitor which delivered specific capacitance of 268 F/g.[61] CNT/MnO_2 core shell based supercapacitor showed two times higher specific capacitance than MnO_2. Fan's group has reported several with 1D core–shell heterostructures such as Co_3O_4/NiO, Co_3O_4/MnO_2, $Co_3O_4/PEDOT//MnO_2CoO/NiHON$, CoO/TiO_2. The Co_3O_4/MnO_2 core–shell heterostructures delivered specific capacitance of 480 F/g at 2.67 A/g. Due to improved electronic conductivity of $NiCo_2O_4$ than Co_3O_4 Liu's group used $NiCo_2O_4$ instead of Co_3O_4. The $NiCo_2O_4/Ni_xCo_{1-x}(OH)_2$ core–shell has obtained specific capacitance up to 1500 F/g with 67% retention. Similarly, $Co_3O_4@PANI$, $V_2O_5@PPy$, $V_2O_5@PEDOT–MnO_2$, $MnO_2@PEDOT–PSS$, $MnO_2@PPy$ have been shows better electrochemical performance than metal oxides like MnO_2, V_2O_5, Co_3O_4 because core shell structures prevent the dissolution problems after cycling.[62,28] The protecting coating thickness and electrochemical performance are related to each other, protecting coating can prevent the dissolution issues but with the increasing thickness accessibility of ions also decreases. So, further study should need to resolve this problem.

2.4.1.3 Two dimensional nanomaterials (2-D)

The sheets or flakes like nanostructure with high aspect ratio are defined as two dimensional nanostructures. 2-D materials exhibited large specific surface area, mechanical and chemical stability, excellent electrical conductivity, due to those unique properties 2-D materials becomes promising candidates for supercapacitor application. In the 2-D nanostructure greater contact area with the electrolytes for utilization of active materials also plays an anchoring role to enhance the electrochemical performance. Like 1-D nanostructure, 2-D nanostructures also have two main categories, named as homostructures and heterostructures.

2.4.1.3.a 2-D Homostructures

The 2-D homostructured electrode materials can classified in to three main subcategories as following

(1) Graphene as active materials for EDLC.

(2) Transition metal oxides and hydroxides as active material for pseudocapacitor.

(3) Transition metal dichalcogenides (TMDs) and transition metal carbides and/or nitrides (MXenes).

2.4.1.3.a (i)Graphene

Among the different forms of carbon, 2-D graphene have been broadly used electrode materials of supercapacitors. In the year of 2004, monolayer of sp^2 bonded carbon atoms in a 2-D honeycomb lattice (Graphene) was experimentally discovered by K.S. Novoselvo and co-workers.[63] Now a day, Graphene is one of the most common active materials in field of energy storage its provides larger theoretical specific surface area (2630 m^2/g), high mechanical and chemical strength and extremely high electronic conductivity.[64] However, restacking properties of graphene sheets plays a negative role due to which graphene based supercapacitors does not provides expected results. The theoretical value of the graphene based supercapacitor is 550F/g whereas reported values are in the range from 80 to 118 F/g.[65] Due to the hydrophilic nature of the chemically synthesized reduced graphene oxides (rGO) for presence of functional groups on rGO the production of composites with metal oxides becomes much easier. Further modification can also be done by adding other functional groups on rGO, which serve as the redox centres. Ruoff et al. have produced chemically modified graphene (CMG) with a specific surface area 705m^2/g. The resulting CMG based supercapacitor showed specific capacitance of 135F/g in aqueous electrolyte and that 99F/g in presence of organic electrolyte.[65] Ruoff and co-workers reported the synthesis the activated rGO using KOH in GO with a specific surface area of 3100 m^2/g. The resulting activated graphene delivered high specific capacitance of 166 F/g at a current density of 5.7 A/g and ~ 97% of the capacitance retention after 10000 cycles.[64] Vacuum low-temperature exfoliated graphene based supercapacitor showed specific capacitance of 220 F/g and 120 F/g in presence of aqueous and organic electrolytes respectively.[66] The rGO prepared by thermal treatment at 200°C from GO also delivered a specific capacitance of 122 F/g at 5 mA.[67] El-Kady et al. reported laser-treated well aligned laser-scribed graphene (LSG) obtained using a standard Light Scribe CD/DVD optical drive. Cross sectional The supercapacitor based on the LSG sheets delivered enhanced electrochemical performance than the other graphene-based flexible supercapacitors.[68]

2.4.1.3.a (ii) Metal oxides and hydroxides

2-D transition metal oxides such as MnO_2, RuO_2, MoO_3, NiO, V_2O_5, Co_2O_3, IrO_2, and SnO_2 are played an important role to development of hybrid supercapacitors. Table 1 shows the theoretical specific capacitance of some transition metal oxides. Though, the practical specific capacitances of those metal oxides are far behind the theoretical value due to the low electrical conductivity. Kang and co-workers reported 2D MnO_2 prepared by soft template technique, exhibited a high specific capacitance of 774 F/g.[69] RuO_2 thin films supercapacitor delivered specific capacitance up to 730 F/g.[70]

2.4.1.3.a (iii) Transition metal dichalcogenides (TMDs)

Recently, layered TMDS like MoS_2, TiS_2, WS_2, and VS_2 have taken attention due to their prospective applications such as sensor, opto-electronics and electrode of SC. The shortcomings of graphene could easily overcome due to the unique properties of TMDs. Among TMDS, MoS_2 have taken the most attention than other because of its intrinsic conductivity and predicted greater theoretical capacity than graphene.[71,72] Edge-oriented MoS_2 films micro-supercapacitor reported by Soon and co-workers showed CNT electrodes like electrochemical performance.[73,74] Geng and co-workers reported flower-like MoS_2 electrode material exhibited a specific capacitance of 168 F/g with 93% capacitance retention after 3000 cycles. Feng and co-worker reported in plane supercapacitor by layered VS_2, which was exhibited specific capacitance of 4760 $\mu F/cm^2$ with 90 % capacitance retention after 1000 cycles.[75]

2.4.1.3.a (iv)Transition metal carbides and/or nitrides (MXenes) nanostructure

A new promising candidate for supercapacitors consisting highly 2-D conductive carbide and carbonitride layers with a hydrophilic, primarily hydroxyl-terminated surface labelled as MXenes was recently introduced by Gogotsi and his team. MXenes based supercapacitor offered high capacitance (300 F/cm^3) more than that of porous carbon, due to the cations (Li^+, Mg^{2+}, Al^{3+}, Cs^+, K^+, NH^{4+}, Na^+, Ba^{2+}, Ca^{2+}) intercalation.[76,77] 2-D MXenes are derived from layered hexagonal carbides or carbonitrides (MAX phases) by removing A layers from it. In the formula of $M_{n+1}AX_n$ (n = 1, 2, 3), M signifies an early transition metals (e.g. Ti, V, Cr, Nb, etc.), A represents IIIA or IVA elements (e.g. Ga, Al, Si, Sn, In or Ge); and X represents C and/or N. Till now, only eleven MXenes are tested experimentally though variety of

MXenes predicted theoretically.[78,79] Lukatskaya and co-worker reported $Ti_3C_2T_x$ MXene material based supercapacitor which showed 350 F/cm^3 volumetric capacitance in presence of aqueous NaOH electrolyte.[76]

2.4.1.3.b 2-D heterostructures

The electrochemical performances of the 2-D homostructures is enhanced after formation of 2-D heterostructures, these is due to the fact that the electrical conductivity, thermal stability and mechanical strength of the composites or hybrid electrode materials are improved than 2-D homostructures.

2.4.1.3.b (i)Graphene/metal oxides and hydroxides hybrids or nanocomposites

Graphene have potential application as an electrode material of EDLC. The Graphene/ TMOs and Graphene/hydroxides hybrids offer both pseudo capacitance and EDLC contribution, which enriched the performance of supercapacitor. RuO_2/graphene hybrid containing 30 wt% graphene sheets exhibited specific capacitance of 370 F/g at 2mV/s.[80]Zhang and co-worker reported rGO/RuO_2 hybrid delivered maximum specific capacitance of 357 F/g at a current density of 0.3 A/g.[81].Graphene/MnO_2 hybrid synthesized by microwave irradiation offered specific capacitance of 310 F/g at 2 mV/s with 95 % capacitance retention after 15000 cycles test.[82] Dong et.al reported Co–Al hydroxide nanosheets/graphene based supercapacitor delivered 880 F/g specific capacitance at 5 mV/s with 99% capacitance retention after 2000 cycles.[83] $Ni(OH)_2$ nanosheet/ Graphene exhibited specific capacitance of 660.8 F/cm^3, which also offered 98.2% capacitance retention after 2000 cycles.[84] Other metal oxides (such as ZnO, Fe_3O_4, SnO_2) hybrids with graphene also offered improved performance.[85-87]

2.4.1.3.b (ii) Graphene-dichalcogenides

Like TMOs, layered TMDs also used widely in the field of energy conversion and energy storage due to its decent electrocatalytic performance, high chemical stability, low cost. Besides of that, layered structure of the TMDs also helpful for the insert and remove of electrolyte ions. But the poor cycle stability and low conductivity limits its practical application in the energy storage field. Graphene/TMDs hybrids are offers improved electrochemical performance with good chemical stability and enriched conductivity due to graphene addition. Rout and co-worker reported hydrothermally synthesized WS_2/rGO hybrid electrode material, which exhibited specific capacitance of 350 F/g at 2 millivolt per sec scan rate.[88] E.G.da Silveira and his team investigated the electrochemical performance of MoS_2/rGO hybrid. The hybrid exhibited 265 F/g specific capacitance at 10 mV/sec scan rate and 92% capacitance retention after 1000 cycles.[89]

2.4.1.3.b (iii)Graphene /2D transition metal carbides and vanadyl phosphate

Zhao and co-worker investigated the electrochemical properties of 2-D Titanium carbide ($Ti_3C_2T_x$)/rGO composites, with different wt% of rGO. The obtained maximum specific capacitance was 154.3 F/g at 2A/g with 85% capacitance retention after 6000 cycles. Gogotsi et.al reported free standing $Ti_3C_2T_x$/rGO electrode, which revealed a volumetric capacitance of 1040 F/cm^3 at 2 mV/s scan rate. Layered VOPO$_4$/graphene hybrid based flexible supercapacitor exhibited areal capacitance of 8360.5 mF/cm^2 and 96% capacitance retention after 2000 cycles[90]

2.4.1.4 Three dimensional nanomaterials (3-D)

3-D nanomaterials are made of low dimensional building block. Carbon nanofoams or sponges and nickel foam are serving as extremely porous and conductive templates on which metal oxides, polymers, graphene; CNTs can be deposited to form 3D nanostructures for supercapacitor electrode. 3-D nanomaterials provides large specific surface and well defined path to access electrolyte ions due to its porous structure.[91-96] Xie and co-worker reported MnO_2-coated 3D grapheme exhibits specific capacitance of 130 F/g and showed 82% capacitance retention after 5000 cycles.[97] The asymmetric supercapacitor fabricated by $Ni_{0.61}Co_{0.39}$ oxide on nickel foam exhibited a specific capacitance of 1523 F/g at 2 A/g current density, where the used electrode acted.as a positive electrode with activated carbon as a negative electrode. The asymmetric supercapacitor also obtained high energy density of 36.46 W h/ kg at a power density 142 W/kg and 95% capacitance retention after 1000 cycles.[98] Zhou and co-worker reported CoO–PPy on 3D nickel foam based supercapacitor, which showed specific capacitance of 2223 F/ g at 1 mA/cm^2.[99]

2.4.1.5 Advantages of 2-D materials

Among different nanostructures, two dimensional nano materials become attractive electrode materials to achieve the flexible supercapacitors. And this is due to their unique properties such as

a. 2-D nanomaterials provide large specific surface area.

b. It provides macro mechanical flexibility to form thin films.

c. Atomically thick layer 2-D materials have high electrochemical active sites.

d. Moreover, 2-D materials possess confined thickness, which provide well-behaved electrical properties also.

2.4.2 Electrolyte for Supercapacitor

The electrolyte also played an important role for the development of ECs. Electrolytes are one of the important components of SCs, providing ionic conductivity. The performance of electrochemical capacitor is directly influenced by the size and nature of the electrolyte ions, concentration of ions, electrolyte/electrode materials interaction and electrochemical stable potential window (ESPW) of the electrolytes. During the past several decades, various types of electrolytes have been already introduced and each electrolyte has its own advantages and drawbacks. The electrolytes are classified as: (a) Liquid electrolytes, (b) Solid state / quasi-solid state electrolytes and as shown in the figure 2.6.

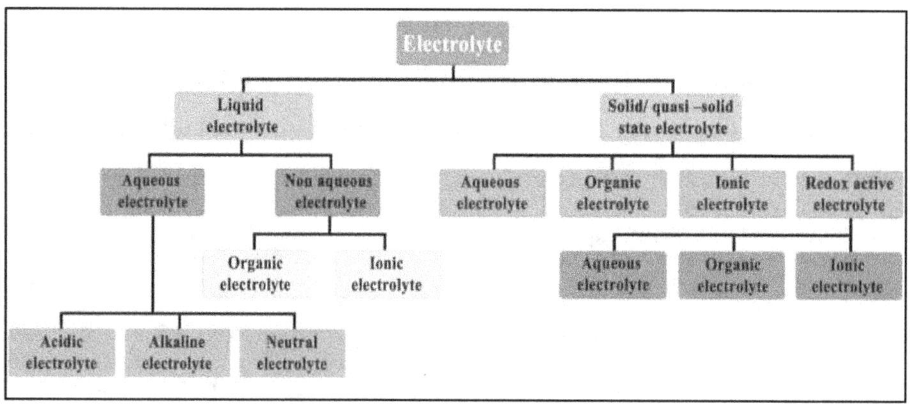

Figure 2.6 Types of electrolytes for supercapacitors.

2.4.2.1 Liquid electrolytes

Liquid electrolytes can be broadly divided into three main sub grouped named as (i) aqueous electrolytes,(ii) organic electrolytes and (iii) ionic electrolytes. Aqueous electrolytes provide high conductivity but low electrochemical stable potential window (ESPW) whereas organic and ionic electrolytes possess high ESPW but struggle with low ionic conductivity. In addition, potential leakage problem of the liquid electrolytes can be resolved by replacing it with solid electrolyte, but they also suffer from low ionic conductivity.

2.4.2.1 a. Aqueous electrolytes

For the improvement of energy density of supercapacitors, aqueous electrolytes are poor choice due to its low potential window. However, aqueous electrolytes have been used widely in research because of its low cost and easily handled nature than organic and ionic electrolytes. Besides of that aqueous electrolytes also offered high conductivity than other liquid electrolytes, which is beneficial to enhance power delivery and dropping the equivalent series resistance (ESR) of ECSs. The ionic conductivity of the different aqueous electrolytes are shown in the table (2.1).[100-104]

Table 2.1 Ionic conductivity, sizes of the bare and hydrated cations and anions of ions

Ion	Bare ion size (Å)	Hydrated ion size(Å)	Ionic Conductivity (S cm^2 mol^{-1})
H^+	1.15	2.80	350.1
K^+	1.33	3.31	73.5
Li^+	0.60	3.82	38.69
Mg^{2+}	0.72	4.28	106.12
Na^+	0.95	3.58	50.11
Ca^{2+}	1.00	4.12	119
SO_4^{2-}	2.90	3.79	160.0
OH^-	1.76	3.00	198
Cl^-	1.35	4.04	127.8
PO_4^{3-}	2.23	3.39	207
CO_3^{2-}	2.66	3.94	138.6

There are mainly three types of aqueous electrolytes named as acidic aqueous electrolytes, alkaline aqueous electrolytes and neutral aqueous electrolytes. 1M H_2SO_4 electrolyte with ionic conductivity 0.8 Scm^{-1} at room temperature is most frequently used acidic electrolyte.[105] The acidic aqueous electrolytes widely used for EDLCs. Besides of acidic electrolytes, KOH, NaOH and LiOH etc. have also been studied as alkaline aqueous electrolytes and among them 6M KOH has exhibited maximum ionic conductivity (0.6 S/cm at 25°C). These alkaline electrolytes can be used for all three types of electrode materials. It can be reported that maximum limiting voltage is 1.3V for both acidic and alkaline electrolytes, independent on the nature of the electrode materials used for ECSs, whereas reported maximum cell voltage is 2.2 V for the neutral electrolyte.[106,107] LiCl, Li_2SO_4, Na_2SO_4, NaCl, K_2SO_4, KCl, $MgSO_4$ etc. are previously reported neutral electrolyte, which are generally used in pseudocapacitors () and hybrid capacitors(HSCs). Among different neutral electrolytes Na_2SO_4 is frequently used for PSCs. Some previously reported aqueous electrolyte-based ECSs and their performance are shown in the table.

Table 2.2 Table of previously reported aqueous electrolyte-based ECSs and their performance

Aqueous Electrolyte	Electrode materials	Specific capacitance (F/g)	Energy density (Wh/kg)	Power density (W/kg)	Ref.
Strong acid electrolyte:					
1M H_2 SO_4	Graphene/mPANI	749 at 0.5 A/ g	11.3	106.7	108
1 M H_2SO_4	AC fibers	280 at 0.5 A /g			109
2 M H_2SO_4	carbon nanofiber networks	204.9 at 1 A/ g	7.76	~100	110
0.5M H_2SO_4	RuO_2–graphene	479 at 0.25 A/ g	20.28	600	111
1 M H_2SO_4	PANI-grafted rGO	1045.51 at 0.2 A/ g	8.3	60000	112
Strong alkaline electrolyte:					
2 M KOH	sub-3 nm Co_3O_4 Nanofilms	1400 at 1 A/ g	-	-	113
1 M LiOH	MnO_2 nanoflower	363 at 2mV /s	-	-	114
6 M KOH	highly porous graphene planes	303 at 0.5 A/ g	-	-	115
6 M KOH	p-CNTn/CGBs	202 at 0.325 A/ g	4.9	150	116
Neutral electrolyte:					
0.5 M Na_2SO_4	seaweed carbons	123 at 0.2 A/ g	10.8	-	117
1M $NaNO_3$	AC	116 at 2mV /s	-	-	118
4 M $NaNO_3$– EG	AC	22.3 at 2 mV/ s	14–16	~500	119
1 M KCl	$MnCl_2$-doped PANI/SWCNT	546 at 0.5 A/ g	194.13	550	118
1M Na_2SO_3	well-ordered mesoporous carbon/Fe_2O_3	235 at 0.5 A/ g	39.4	-	119

2.4.2.1 b. Non-aqueous electrolytes

The non-aqueous organic and ionic electrolytes were employed to overcome the potential barrier (up to 3.5 V) over the aqueous electrolyte. The higher operation cell potential can provide an improved energy and power densities. Triethylmethylammonium tetrafluoroborate and tetraethylammonium tetrafluoroborate in acetonitrile are mostly used organic electrolyte, which provides a comparatively larger potential window around 2-2.5 V. Organic electrolytes have a larger cost, lower conductivity and also requires complicated purification before use. It has been already reported that the electrochemical performance of activated carbon is poorer in organic electrolytes (50-150 F/g) than in aqueous electrolytes (100-300 F/g).[120,121] This is due the fact that, effective ions size of the electrolyte in organic solutions is much larger than those in water. Moreover, the disadvantages like electrolyte depletion upon charge and safety concerns related to the toxicity, instability also bound the use of organic electrolytes. Some previously reported organic electrolytes performances are shown in the table 2.3. Ionic liquids, a type of organic salts (molten salts) have many potential advantages like wide ESPW, high thermal, chemical and electrochemical stability; non-flammability. Additionally, depending on the requirements of electrochemical performances like operating cell voltage, working temperature etc. compositions of the electrolytes can also be optimized or customized due to its highly tunable physical and chemical properties. Low ionic conductivity at room temperature, high viscosity limits its application, so ionic liquids are mainly used at high temperature. Ionic liquids are completely composed of cations and anions. Tetrafluoroborate (BF_4^-), hexafluorophosphate (PF_6) bis (trifluoromethanesulfonyl) imide ($TFSI^-$), bis(fluorosulfonyl)imide (FSI^-), and dicyanamide (DCA^-) are the commonly used anions of ILs whereas imidazolium, pyrrolidinium, ammonium, sulfonium, phosphonium commonly used cations. Balducci and co-worker reported N-butyl-N-methylpyrrolidinium bis(trifluoromethanesulfonyl)imide ionic liquid filled AC supercapacitor, which delivered a C_{sp} of 60 F/g with high cycling stability for 40000 cycles. G. Yushin and co-worker reported polypyrrole-derived activated carbon based symmetric EDLC with $EMImBF_4$ ionic liquid electrolyte showed a specific capacitance of 300 F/g. Among the several ILs, [EMIM][BF 4] electrolyte have higher conductivity (14 mS/cm at 25°C).But it is much lower than $TEABF_4$ /CAN (59.9 mS /cm at 25°C) organic electrolyte. The improvement of ionic liquid for ES applications is still in the initial stage and progress is required to ensure their full utilization.

Table 2.3 Table of previously reported organic electrolyte-based ECSs and their performance

Electrolyte	Electrode materials	Specific capacitance (F/g)	Energy density (Wh/kg)	Power density (W/k)	Ref.
1 M TEABF 4 /ACN	highly porous interconnected carbon nanosheets	120–150 at 1 mV s −1	25	25000–27000	120
1 M TEABF 4 /HFIP	AC	110 at 1 mV s −1	-	-	121
0.7 M TEABF 4 /ADN	AC	25 at 20 mV s −1	~28		122
1 M TEABF 4 /PC	graphene–CNT composites	110 at 1 A g −1	34.3	400	123
MC-PC-EA	Microporous carbide derived carbon	120 at 1 mV s −1	40	90	124
0.5 M Bu 4 NBF 4 /ACN	H-carbazol-9-yl acetic acid)/TiO_2 nanoparticles composite	462.88 at 2.5 mA cm −	89.98	-	125
1.5 M TEMABF 4 /PC	mesophase carbon microbeads/ graphitized carbon	363 at 2mV /s	60	~30	112
1 M LiTFSI/ACN	MnO_2 nanorodes– rGO//V_2O_5 NWs–rGO	36.9	15.4	436.5	126
1 M LiPF 6 /EC-DMC(1:1)	Commercial AC (MSP-20)//mesoporous Nb_2O_5 – carbon nanocomposite	202 at 0.325 A/ g	74	~100	127
1 M LiPF 6 /(EC-DEC 1:1):	Nanoporous Co_3O_4 – graphene composites	123 at 0.2 A/g	-	-	128

2.4.2.2 Solid- or quasi-solid-state electrolytes

Now a days, solid-state or quasi solid state electrolyte based supercapacitors take tremendous attention to develop the flexible portable devices. The solid-state electrolytes plays duel role in flexible supercapacitors such as ionic conducting media and the electrode separators due to which, leakage free flexible device can easily achieved. The performance of flexible supercapacitors depends on a solid state electrolyte that shows good mechanical and chemical stability with high ionic conductivity. Generally, gel electrolyte are composed of polymer, such as polyvinyl alcohol (PVA), polyvinylpyrrolidone (PVP), polyethylene glycol (PEO) and polypolyacrylate (PAA) etc. with a proton conducting aqueous solutions. Table 2.4 presents the typical solid state electrolyte-based ECS's performance.

Table 2.4 Ionic conductivity of solid state electrolyte

Electrolyte	Type of electrolyte	Ionic conductivity ($S\ cm^2\ mol^{-1}$)	Ref.
PVA/H_2SO_4	Aqueous	30	129
PVA/KOH	Aqueous	0.1	130
PAM/LiCl	Aqueous	10	131
PAA/TEAOH	Aqueous	0.9	132
PVA/GO doped KOH	Aqueous	200	133
$PEO/LiCO_4\text{-}TiO_2\text{-}Al_2O_3$	Organic	0.03	134
PEO/PC-NaTFSI	Organic	0.54	135
$PVDF\text{-}HFP/PC\text{-}Mg(ClO_4)_2$	Organic	5.4	136
$PAN\text{-}b\text{-}PEG\text{-}b\text{-}PAN/LiClO_4$	Organic	11	137
PVA/BMIMCl-LiClO4	Ionic	37	138
$PEO/EMIHSO_4\text{-}MIHSO_4$	Ionic	1.7	139
$PEO/\ EMIHSO_4\text{-}ImHSO_4$	Ionic	2.5	139
PEGDA/EMIMTFSI	Ionic	9.4	140
PHEMA-chitosan/EMIMCl	Ionic	25	141
PVA/p-Benzenediol(PB) doped H_2SO_4	Redox active aqueous	34.8	142
PVA/BAAS doped H_2SO_4	Redox active aqueous	21.4	143
PVA/AQQS doped H_2SO_4	Redox active aqueous	28.5	144
PMMA/PC-Fc doped $TEABF_4$	Redox active organic	1.89	145
PMMA/PC 4-oxo TEMPO doped $TEABF_4$	Redox active organic	1.73	145
$PVA/EMIMBF_4$ doped H_3PO_4	Redox active ionic	39.3	143

2.5. References

1. Wikipedia, Wikipedia, http://en.wikipedia.org /wiki/Electric_double-layer_capacitor

2. B.E Conway, Electrochemical Supercapacitors: Scientific Fundamentals and Technological Applications, Kluwer academic/ Plenum publishers, 1999, pp17-556

3. J. Garthwaite," Supercapacitor Market to Surge to $877M by 2014", http://earth2tech.com /2009/06/10/supercapacitor-market-to-surge-to-877m-by-2014/.

4. L. Sibley, "Researchers See Spike in Supercapacitor Demand", Cleantech Group, 2009, http://cleantech.com/news/4576/rese +/.*B&/(B)+H)B $(+1 B)=C$/.+C+.]

5. Nano Markets, "Market for Battery and Supercapacitor Storage Systems for Smart Grid Applications Expect to reach $8.3 Billion in 2016", http://www.azonano.com/ news.asp? newsID=12902.

6. Y. Wang, Z. Shi, Y. Huang, Y. Ma, C. Wang, M. Chen and Y. Chen, *J. Phys. Chem. C,* 2009, **113**, 13103–13107.

7. J. Huang, B. G. Sumpter and V. Meunier, *Angew. Chem., Int. Ed.*, 2008, **47**, 520–524

8. J. Gamby, P. Taberna, P. Simon, J. Fauvarque and M. Chesneau, *J. Power Sources,* 2001, **101**, 109–116.

9. D. N. Futaba, K. Hata, T. Yamada, T. Hiraoka, Y. Hayamizu,Y. Kakudate, O. Tanaike, H. Hatori, M. Yumura and S. Iijima, *Nat. Mater.,* 2006, **5**, 987–994.

10. L. L. Zhang, R. Zhou and X. Zhao, J. *Mater. Chem,,.* 2010, **20**, 5983–5992.

11. W. Tang, L. Liu, S. Tian, L. Li, Y. Yue, Y. Wu and K. Zhu, *Chem. Commun.*, 2011 **47**, 10058-10060.

12. F. Luan, G. Wang, Y. Ling, X. Lu, H. Wang, Y. Tong, X.X. Liu and Y. Li, *Nanoscale,* 2013, **5**, 7984-7990.

13. C.C. Hu, K.H. Chang, M.C. Lin and Y.T. Wu, *Nano Lett.,* 2006, **6**, 2690-2695.

14. X. Lu, G. Wang, T. Zhai, M. Yu, J. Gan, Y. Tong and Y. Li, *Nano Lett.,* 2012, **12**, 1690-1696.

15. X. Lu, T. Zhai, X. Zhang, Y. Shen, L. Yuan, B. Hu, L. Gong, J. Chen, Y. Gao, J. Zhou, Y. Tong and Z. L. Wang, *Adv. Mater.,* 2012, **24**, 938-944.

16. G. Yu, L. Hu, N. Liu, H. Wang, M. Vosgueritchian, Y. Yang, Y. Cui and Z. Bao, *Nano Lett.,*2011, **11**, 4438-4442.

17. G. Yu, L. Hu, M. Vosgueritchian, H. Wang, X. Xie, J. R. McDonough, X. Cui, Y. Cui and Z. Bao, *Nano Lett.,* 2011, **11**, 2905-2911.

18. L. Wu, R. Li, J. Guo, C. Zhou, W. Zhang, C. Wang, Y. Huang, Y. Li and J. Liu, *AIP Adv.,*2013, **3**, 082129.

19. L. Peng, X. Peng, B. Liu, C. Wu, Y. Xie and G. Yu, *Nano Lett.,*2013, **13**, 2151-2157.

20. J. Feng, X. Sun, C. Wu, L. Peng, C. Lin, S. Hu, J. Yang and Y. Xie, *J. Am. Chem. Soc.,* 2011, **133**, 17832-17838.

21. J. Xie, X. Sun, N. Zhang, K. Xu, M. Zhou and Y. Xie, *Nano Energy* ,2013**, 2**, 65-74.

22. J. Yan, Z. Fan, W. Sun, G. Ning, T. Wei, Q. Zhang, R. Zhang, L. Zhi and F. Wei, *Adv. Funct. Mater,.*2012, **22**, 2632-2641.

23. V. Gupta, T. Kusahara, H. Toyama, S. Gupta and N. Miura, *Electrochem. Commun.* ,2012, **9**, 2315-2319.

24. H. Wang, Q. Hao, X. Yang, L. Lu and X. Wang, *Nanoscale* 2010, **2**, 2164-2170.

25. K. Jurewicz, S. Delpeux, V. Bertagna, F. Beguin and E. Frackowiak, *Chem. Phys. Lett.,* 2001, **347**, 36-40.

26. J. Tao, N. Liu, W. Ma, L. Ding, L. Li, J. Su and Y. Gao, *Sci. Rep.,* 2013, **3**, 2286.

27. A. Laforgue, P. Simon, C. Sarrazin, J. F. Fauvarque, *J. Power Sources,* 1999, **80**, 142-148.

28. Z.Yu, L. Tetard, L.Zhai and Jayan Thomas, Energy Environ. Sci., 2015, 8, 702-730.

29. C. Lin, J. A. Ritter and B. N. Popov, *J. Electrochem. Soc.*, 1999, **146**, 3155-3160.

30. K. Lota, A. Sierczynska and G. Lota, *Int. J. Electrochem.,* 2011, **2011**, 321473.

31. M. P. Yeager, D. Su, N. S. Marinkovic and X. Teng, *J. Electrochem. Soc.*, 2012, **159**, A1598-A1603.

32. Y.Z. Zheng, H.Y. Ding and M.L. Zhang, *Mater. Res. Bull.,*2009, **44**, 403-407.

33. X. Du, C. Wang, M. Chen, Y. Jiao and J. Wang, J. *Phys. Chem. C*, 2009, **113**, 2643-2646.

34. L. Hu, W. Wang, J. Tu, J. Hou, H. Zhu and S. Jiao, *J. Mater. Chem. A*, 2013, **1**, 5136-5141.

35. C. Liu, F. Li, L. P. Ma and H. M. Cheng, *Adv. Mater.*, 2010, **22**, E28-E62.]

36. C. Portet, G. Yushin and Y. Gogotsi, Carbon, 2007, **45**, 2511-2518.

37. D. Pech, M. Brunet, H. Durou, P. Huang, V. Mochalin,Y. Gogotsi, P.L. Taberna and P. Simon, *Nat. Nanotechnol.*, 2010, **5**, 651–654

38. X. Lang, A. Hirata, T. Fujita and M. Chen, *Nat. Nanotechnol.*, 2011, **6**, 232–236

39. J. T. Me ff ord, W. G. Hardin, S. Dai, K. P. Johnston and K. J. Stevenson, *Nat. Mater.*, 2014, **13**, 726-732.

40. .B. You, J. Yang, Y. Sun and Q. Su, *Chem. Commun.*, 2011, **47**, 12364-12366.

41. X. Tang, Z.-h. Liu, C. Zhang, Z. Yang and Z. Wang, J. Power Sources, 2009, 193, 939-943.

42. S.-W. Bian, Y.P. Zhao and C.Y. Xian, Mater. Lett., 2013, 111,75-77.

43. C.Y. Cao, W. Guo, Z.M. Cui, W.G. Song and W. Cai, *J.Mater. Chem.*, 2011, **21**, 3204-3209.

44. W. Yu, X. Jiang, S. Ding and B. Q. Li, *J. Power Sources*, 2014, **256**, 440-448.

45. Z. Yang, F. Xu, W. Zhang, Z. Mei, B. Pei and X. Zhu, *J. Power Sources*, 2014, **246**, 24-31.

46. Y. Wang, A. Pan, Q. Zhu, Z. Nie, Y. Zhang, Y. Tang, S. Liang and G. Cao, *J. Power Sources*, 2014, **272**, 107-112.

47. X. Lai, J. Li, B. A. Korgel, Z. Dong, Z. Li, F. Su, J. Du and D.Wang, *Angew. Chem., Int. Ed.*, 2011, **50**, 2738-2741.

48. Z. Yang, F. Xu, W. Zhang, Z. Mei, B. Pei and X. Zhu, *J. Power Sources*, 2014, **246**, 24–31.

49. Z. Lei, Z. Chen and X. Zhao, *J. Phys. Chem. C*, 2010, **114**, 19867-19874.

50. Z. Lei, J. Zhang and X. Zhao, *J. Mater. Chem.*, 2012, **22**, 153–160.

51. L. Fan, L. Tang, H. Gong, Z. Yao and R. Guo, *J. Mater. Chem.*,2012, **22**, 16376-16381.

52. Z. Lei, Z. Chen and X. Zhao, *J. Phys. Chem. C*, 2010, **114**, 19867-19874.

53. B. Duong, Z. Yu, P. Gangopadhyay, S. Seraphin, N. Peyghambarian and J. Thomas, Adv. Mater. Interfaces, 2014, 1, 1300014.

54. X. Lu, Y. Zeng, M. Yu, T. Zhai, C. Liang, S. Xie, M. S. Balogun and Y. Tong, Adv. Mater., 2014, 26, 3148–3155.

55. G.Y. Zhao and H.L. Li, *Microporous Mesoporous Mater.*, 2008, **110**, 590–594.

56. Y.Y. Horng, Y.C. Lu, Y.K. Hsu, C.C. Chen, L.C. Chen and K.H. Chen, J. *Power Sources*, 2010, **195**, 4418–4422.

57. G. Q. Zhang, H. B. Wu, H. E. Hoster, M. B. Chan-Park and X. W. D. Lou, *Energy Environ. Sci.*, 2012, 5, 9453–9456.

58. H. Xia, J. Feng, H. Wang, M. O. Lai and L. Lu, *J. Power Sources*, 2010, 195, 4410–4413.

59. .C.C. Hu, K.H. Chang, M.C. Lin and Y.T. Wu, *Nano Lett.*, 2006, 6, 2690–2695.

60. H. Pan, J. Y. Li and Y. P. Feng, *Nanoscale Res. Lett.*, 2010, **5**, 654–668.

61. R. K. Sharma, A. Karakoti, S. Seal and L. Zhai, *J. Power Sources*, 2010, **195**, 1256–1262.

62. C. Guan, J. Liu, C. Cheng, H. Li, X. Li, W. Zhou, H. Zhang and H. J. Fan, Energy Environ. Sci., 2011, 4, 4496–4499.

63. K.S. Novoselov, A. K. Geim, S. V. Morozov, D. Jiang, Y. Zhang, S. V. Dubonos, I. V. Grigorieva and A. A. Firsov, *Science*, 2004, **306**, 666–669.

64. Y. Zhu, S. Murali, M. D. Stoller, K. J. Ganesh, W. Cai, P. J. Ferreira, A. Pirkle, R.M. Wallace, K. A. Cychosz, M. Thommes, D. Su, E. A. Stach and R. S. Ruoff, *Science*, 2011, **332**, 1537-1541.

65. M. D. Stoller, S. Park, Y. Zhu, J. and R. S. Ruoff, *Nano Lett.* 2008, **8**, 3498-3502.

66. W. Lv, D.-M. Tang, Y.-B. He, C.H. You, Z.Q. Shi, X.-C. Chen, C.-M. Chen, P.X. Hou, C. Liu and Q.H. Yang, *ACS Nano*, 2009, **3**, 3730–3736

67. Y. Zhu, M. D. Stoller, W. Cai, A. Velamakanni, R. D. Piner, D. Chen and R. S. Ruo ff, *ACS Nano*, 2010, **4**, 1227–1233]

68. M. F. ElKady, V. Strong, S. Dubin and R. B. Kaner, *Science*, 2012, **335**, 1326-1330.

69. S. Shi, C. Xu, C. Yang, Y. Chen, J. Liu and F. Kang, *Sci. Rep.*, 2013, **3**, 2598.

70. T. P. Gujar, V. R. Shinde, C. D. Lokhande, W.Y. Kim, K.D. Jung and O.S. Joo, *Electrochem. Commun.*, 2007, **9**, 504-510.

71. L. Cao, S. Yang, W. Gao, Z. Liu, Y. Gong, L. Ma, G. Shi,S. Lei, Y. Zhang, S. Zhang, R. Vajtai and P. M. Ajayan, *Small*, 2013, *9*, 2905-2910.

72. B. Lei, G. R. Li and X. P. Gao, *J. Mater. Chem. A*, 2014, **2**, 3919-3925.

73. X. Wang, J. Ding, S. Yao, X. Wu, Q. Feng, Z. Wang and B. Geng, *J. Mater. Chem. A*, 2014, **2**, 15958–15963.

74. J. M. Soon and K. P. Loh, *Electrochem. Solid-State Lett.*, 2007,**10**, A250-A254.

75. J. Feng, X. Sun, C. Wu, L. Peng, C. Lin, S. Hu, J. Yang and Y. Xie, *J. Am. Chem. Soc.*, 2011, 133, 17832-17838.

76. M. R. Lukatskaya, O. Mashtalir, C. E. Ren, Y. Dall'Agnese, P. Rozier, P. L. Taberna, M. Naguib, P. Simon, M. W. Barsoum and Y. Gogotsi, *Science*, 2013, **341**, 1502-1505.

77. M. Naguib, M. Kurtoglu, V. Presser, J. Lu, J. Niu, M. Heon, L. Hultman, Y. Gogotsi and M. W. Barsoum, *Adv. Mater.*, 2011, **23**, 4248-4253.

78. M. Kurtoglu, M. Naguib, Y. Gogotsi and M. W. Barsoum, *MRS Commun.*, 2012, **2**, 133-137.

79. M. Khazaei, M. Arai, T. Sasaki, C. Y. Chung, N. S. Venkataramanan, M. Estili, Y. Sakka and Y. Kawazoe, *Adv. Funct. Mater.*, 2013, **23**, 2185–2192.

80. H. Wang, Y. Liang, T. Mirfakhrai, Z. Chen, H. Casalongue and H. Dai, *Nano Res.*, 2011, **4**, 729-736.

81. J. Zhang, J. Jiang, H. Li and X. S. Zhao, *Energy Environ. Sci.*, 2011, **4**, 4009-4015.

82. .J. Yan, Z. Fan, T. Wei, W. Qian, M. Zhang and F. Wei, *Carbon*, 2010, **48**, 3825-3833.

83. X. Dong, L. Wang, D. Wang, C. Li and J. Jin, *Langmuir*, 2012, **28**, 293-298.

84. J. Xie, X. Sun, N. Zhang, K. Xu, M. Zhou and Y. Xie, *Nano Energy*, 2013, **2**, 65-74.

85. Q.Qu, S. Yang and X. Feng, *Adv. Mater.*, 2011, **23**, 5574-5580

86. L. Fenghua, S. Jiangfeng, Y. Huafeng, G. Shiyu, Z. Qixian,H. Dongxue, I. Ari and N. Li, *Nanotechnology*, 2009, **20**,455602.

87. Y. Zhang, H. Li, L. Pan, T. Lu and Z. Sun, *J. Electroanal. Chem.*, 2009, **634**, 68–71.

88. S. Ratha and C. S. Rout, *ACS Appl. Mater. Interfaces*, 2013, **5**, 11427–11433.

89. E. G. da Silveira Firmiano, A. C. Rabelo, C. J. Dalmaschio, A. N. Pinheiro, E. C. Pereira, W. H. Schreiner and E. R. Leite, *Adv. Energy Mater.*, 2014, **4**, 1301380

90. .C. Wu, X. Lu, L. Peng, K. Xu, X. Peng, J. Huang, G. Yu and Y. Xie, *Nat. Commun.*, 2013, **4**, 2431.

91. . W. Wang, S. Guo, I. Lee, K. Ahmed, J. Zhong, Z. Favors,F. Zaera, M. Ozkan and C. S. Ozkan, *Sci. Rep.*, 2014, **4**, 4452.

92. Y.M. Wang, X. Zhang, C.Y. Guo, Y.Q. Zhao, C.L. Xu and H.L. Li, *J. Mater. Chem. A*, 2013, **1**, 13290-13300.

93. T. Zhai, F. Wang, M. Yu, S. Xie, C. Liang, C. Li, F. Xiao, R. Tang, Q. Wu, X. Lu and Y. Tong, *Nanoscale*, 2013, **5**, 6790–6796.

94. M. J.Deng, P.J. Ho, C.-Z. Song,S.-A. Chen,J.-F. Lee,J.-M. Chen and K.T. Lu, *Energy Environ. Sci.*, 2013, 6, 2178–2185.

95. X. H. Xia, J. P. Tu, Y. Q. Zhang, Y. J. Mai, X. L. Wang,C. D. Gu and X. B. Zhao, *J. Phys. Chem. C*, 2011, **115**,22662-22668.

96. C. Zhou, Y. Zhang, Y. Li and J. Liu, *Nano Lett.*, 2013, **13**, 2078-2085.

97. Y. He, W. Chen, X. Li, Z. Zhang, J. Fu, C. Zhao and E. Xie, *ACS Nano*, 2013, **7**, 174-182.

98. Y.M. Wang, X. Zhang, C.Y. Guo, Y.Q. Zhao, C.L. Xu and H.L. Li, *J. Mater. Chem. A,* 2013, **1**, 13290–13300.

99. C. Zhou, Y. Zhang, Y. Li and J. Liu, *Nano Lett.*, 2013, 13, 2078-2085

100. .J. G. Speight, Lange's handbook of chemistry, *MCGRAW-HILL,16th edn*, 2005.

101. A. G. Volkov, S. Paula and D. W. Deamer, Bioelectrochem. Bioenerg., 1997, 42, 153–160. E. R. Nightingale, J. Phys. Chem., 1959, 63, 1381-1387.

102. M. Y. Kiriukhin and K. D. Collins, *Biophys. Chem.*, 2002, **99**,155-168.

103. M. Galin´ski, A. Lewandowski and I. Stepniak, *Electrochim. Acta*, 2006, 51, 5567-5580.

104. A. Yu, V. Chabot and J. Zhang, Electrochemical Supercapacitors for Energy Storage and Delivery: Fundamentals and Applications, 2013.

105. K. Fic, G. Lota, M. Meller and E. Frackowiak, *Energy Environ. Sci.*, 2012, **5**, 5842-5850.

106. Q. Wang, J. Yan, Z. J. Fan, T. Wei, M. L. Zhang and X. Y. Jing, *J. Power Sources*, 2014, **247**, 197-203.

107. Z. Jin, X. D. Yan, Y. H. Yu and G. J. Zhao, *J. Mater. Chem. A*, 2014, **2**, 11706–11715.

108. L. F. Chen, Z. H. Huang, H. W. Liang, H. L. Gao and S. H. Yu, *Adv. Funct. Mater.*, 2014, **24**, 5104-5111.

109. L. J. Deng, J. F. Wang, G. Zhu, L. P. Kang, Z. P. Hao, Z. B. Lei, Z. P. Yang and Z. H. Liu, *J. Power Sources*, 2014, **248**, 407-415.

110. X. B. Liu, P. B. Shang, Y. B. Zhang, X. L. Wang, Z. M. Fan, B. X. Wang and Y. Y. Zheng, *J. Mater. Chem. A*, 2014, **2**, 15273-15278.

111. C. Feng, J. F. Zhang, Y. He, C. Zhong, W. B. Hu, L. Liu and Y. D. Deng, *ACS Nano*, 2015, **9**, 1730-1739.

112. I. I. Misnon, R. A. Aziz, N. K. M. Zain, B. Vidhyadharan, S. G. Krishnan and R. Jose, *Mater. Res. Bull.*, 2014, **57**, 221-230.

113. H. J. Wang, X. X. Sun, Z. H. Liu and Z. B. Lei, *Nanoscale*, 2014, **6**, 6577-6584.

114. B. S. Mao, Z. H. Wen, Z. Bo, J. B. Chang, X. K. Huang and J. H. Chen, *ACS Appl. Mater. Interfaces*, 2014, **6**, 9881-9889.

115. M. P. Bichat, E. Raymundo-Pinero and F. Beguin, *Carbon*, 2010, **48**, 4351-4361.

116. Q. Abbas, D. Pajak, E. Frackowiak and F. Beguin, *Electrochim. Acta*, 2014, 140, 132-138.

117. C. Ramasamy, J. P. del Val and M. Anderson, *J. Power Sources*, 2014, **248**, 370-377.

118. S. Dhibar, P. Bhattacharya, G. Hatui, S. Sahoo and C. K. Das, *ACS Sustainable Chem. Eng.*, 2014, **2**, 1114-1127.

119. Y. Lin, X. Y. Wang, G. Qian and J. J. Watkins, *Chem. Mater.*, 2014, **26**, 2128-2137.

120. M. Sevilla and A. B. Fuertes, *ACS Nano*, 2014, 8, 5069-5078.

121. R. Francke, D. Cericola, R. Kotz, D. Weingarth and S. R. Waldvogel, *Electrochim. Acta*, 2012, **62**, 372-380.

122. A. Brandt, P. Isken, A. Lex Balducci and A. Balducci, *J. Power Sources*, 2012, **204**, 213–219.

123. N. Jung, S. Kwon, D. Lee, D. M. Yoon, Y. M. Park, A. Benayad, J. Y. Choi and J. S. Park, *Adv. Mater.*, 2013, **25**, 6854–6858.

124. R. Vali, A. Laheaar, A. Janes and E. Lust, *Electrochim. Acta*, 2014, **121**, 294–300.

125. D. Yigit, M. Gullu, T. Yumak and A. Sinag, *J. Mater. Chem. A*, 2014, 2, 6512–6524.

126. S. D. Perera, M. Rudolph, R. G. Mariano, N. Nijem, J. P. Ferraris, Y. J. Chabal and K. J. Balkus, *Nano Energy*, 2013, **2**, 966-975.

127. E. Lim, H. Kim, C. Jo, J. Chun, K. Ku, S. Kim, H. I. Lee, I. S. Nam, S. Yoon, K. Kang and J. Lee, *ACS Nano*, 2014, **8**, 8968-8978.

128. X. D. Huang, B. Sun, S. Q. Chen and G. X. Wang, *Chem. Asian J.*, 2014, **9**, 206-211.

129. W. Li, T. Li, X. Ma, Y. Li, L. An and Z. Zhang, *RSC Adv.*, 2016, **6**, 12491-12496

130. C. C. Yang, S. T. Hsu and W. C. Chien, J. Power Sources, 2005, 152, 303–310.

131. P. Sivaraman, A. Thakur, R. K. Kushwaha, D. Ratna and A. B. Samui, *Electrochem. Solid-State Lett.*, 2006, **9**, A435–A438.

132. J. Li and K. Lian, *Polymer,* 2016, **99**, 140–146.

133. Y. F. Huang, P. F. Wu, M. Q. Zhang, W. H. Ruan and E. P. Giannelis, *Electrochim. Acta*, 2014, **132**, 103–111.

134. J. K. Lee, Y. J. Lee, W. S. Chae and Y. M. Sung, *J. Electroceram.*, 2006, **17**, 941.

135. C. Ramasamy, J. Palma and M. Anderson, *J. Solid State Electrochem.*, 2014, **18**, 2903-2911.

136. A. Jain and S. K. Tripathi, *Ionics*, 2013, **19**, 549–557.

137. M. F. Hsueh, C. W. Huang, C. A. Wu, P. L. Kuo and H. Teng, *J. Phys. Chem. C*, 2013, **117**, 16751-16758.

138. X. Zhang, L. Wang, J. Peng, P. Cao, X. Cai, J. Li and M. Zhai, *Adv. Mater. Interfaces*, 2015, **2**, 1500267.

139. S. Ketabi, B. Decker and K. Lian, *Sol. State Ionics*, 2016, **298**, 73-79.

140. D. Kim, G. Lee, D. Kim and J. S. Ha, *ACS Appl. Mater. Interfaces*, 2015, 7, 4608-4615

141. X. Liu, D. Wu, H. Wang and Q. Wang, *Adv. Mater.*, 2014, **26**, 4370.

142. F. Miao, C. Shao, X. Li, K. Wang and Y. Liu, *J. Mater. Chem. A*, 2016, **4**, 4180-4187.

143. E. Feng, G. Ma, K. Sun, F. Ran, H. Peng and Z. Lei, *New J. Chem.*, 2017, **41**, 1986–1992.

144. R. Wang, J. Lang, X. Yan, *Science China Chemistry*, 2014, *57*, 1570-1578.

145. C. Zhong, Y.Deng, W. Hu, J. Qiao, L. Zhang and J.Zhang, Chem. Soc. Rev., 2015, 44, 7484-7539.

Chapter 3

Measurement and Characterization Tools

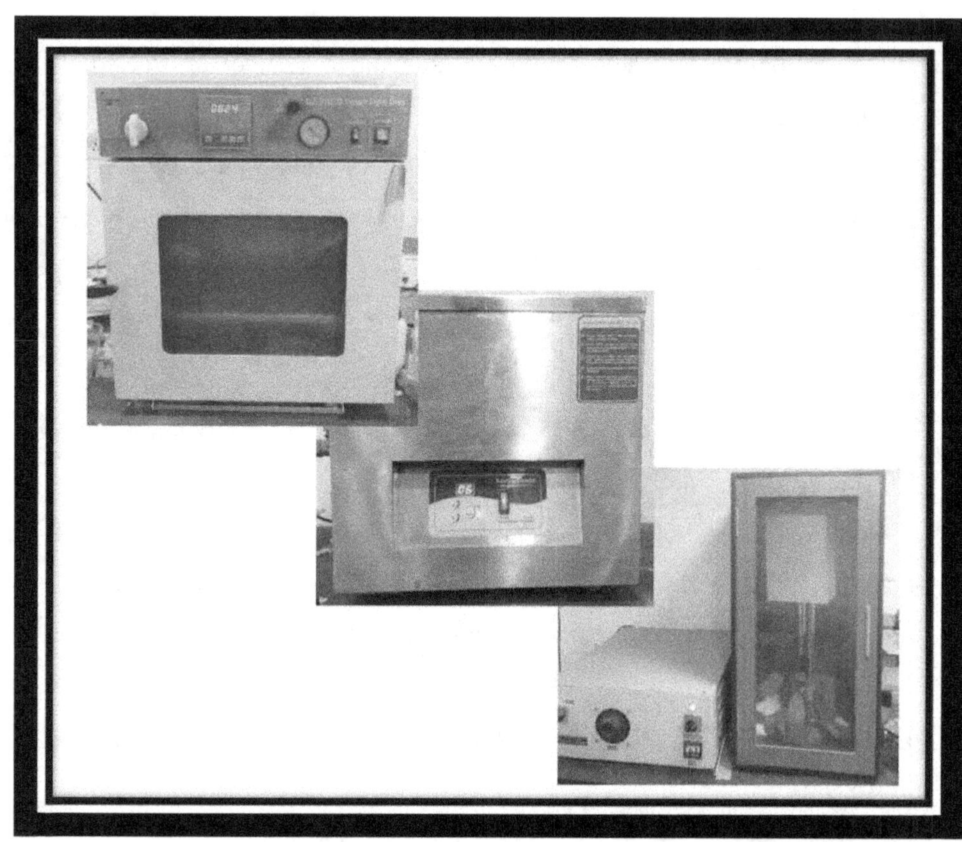

3.1. General Description of Synthesis Apparatus

Mainly liquid phase exfoliation and hydrothermal process were used for the synthesis of the 2-D nanomaterials discussed in this thesis. Following section contain the brief description of these processes. For chemical synthesis of $VOPO_4, 2H_2O$ nanosheets reflux method was used.

3.1.1. Ultra-Sonicator

A horn (high power) sonicator and bath sonicator was used for the liquid phase exfoliation of transition metal oxides (TMOs) from their bulks. Low power bath sonicator was also used for exfoliation of graphene, CNTs and other materials prepared by hydrothermal process for the thin films preparation. Due to the large ultrasonic energy, solvent molecules are oscillates about their mean position at the high frequency ($\sim$ 20 kHz). The shock waves associated with this high frequency oscillation generates large local shear stresses, which breaks the van der Waals bounds of the layered materials. An ultrasonic cleaner was used to clean the substrates (glass, quartz, Si, etc.) using distilled water and preparation of grid required for the HRTEM study. In our lab we have a number of ultra-sonicator as shown in the fig 3.1 with an additional heating arrangement.

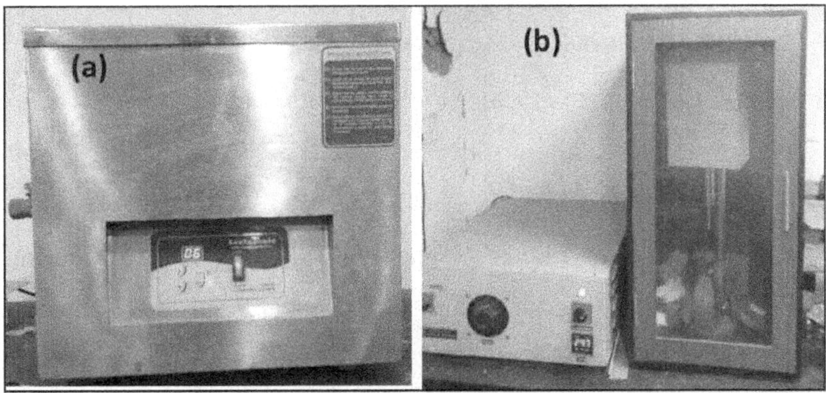

Figure.3.1 Photograph of bath-ultrasonicator(a), Horn-sonicator(b)

3.1.2. Oven and Autoclave

An oven was used for the purpose of performing any hydrothermal reaction. The range of the furnace was up to $500^O C$ and the heating rate can be controlled by an electronic temperature controller with an accuracy of $\pm$ 0.2 $^O C$. The photograph of the used furnace is shown in the Fig. 3.2(a). Hydrothermal synthesis was done using autoclave equipment. An autoclave is a pressurized vessel to heat aqueous solution above their boiling point at a pressure higher than normal pressure. It is basically a cylindrical iron chamber fitted with an iron screw cap. The cap may be fitted very tightly with the iron chamber so that it can withstand a very high pressure during reaction. Synthesis of BiOCl and MoS$_2$ nanosheets through hydrothermal process were done with an autoclave arrangement as shown in Fig. 3.2(b) and (c).

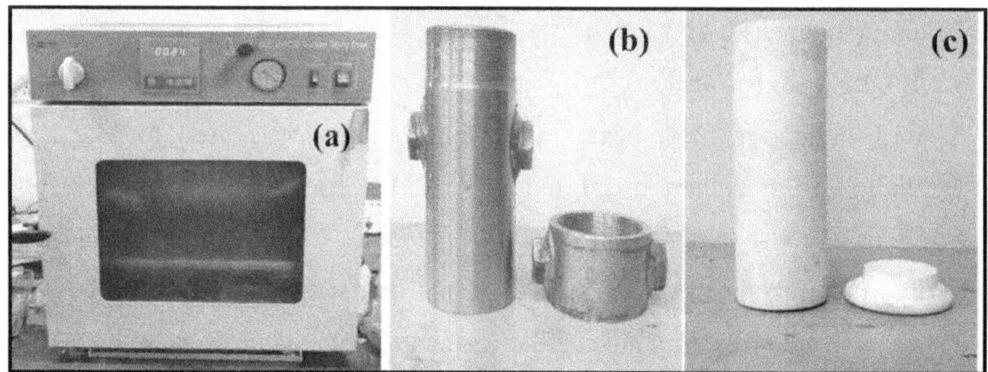

Figure.3.2 *Digital photograph box-furnace and oven (a), Photographs of autoclave jacket (b) and teflon used inside an autoclave(c)*

3.2. Supporting Accessories

The supporting accessories that have been used in the working periods are the following:

3.2.1.   Magnetic Stirrer and Centrifuge

The magnetic stirrer is a very essential supporting apparatus for chemical synthesis. It can stir a magnetic piddle inside the solution of the beaker through a revolving magnetic setup attached with it. The stirrer can also heat the solution at a desired temperature using heater arrangement associated with it as shown in Fig.3.3(a). The hot plate of the stirrer can also use to thin films transfer on different substrates.

 Centrifuge is mainly used to separate impurities from the synthesized products. The rotational speed of the centrifuge can be set up to 18,000 rpm. The photograph of the centrifuge is shown in Fig. 3.3.(b) The synthesis and functionalization of all the carbon structures as well as the synthesis of Mn$_3$O$_4$ nanorods were very much associated with the proper utilization of magnetic stirrer, ultra-sonicator and centrifuge.

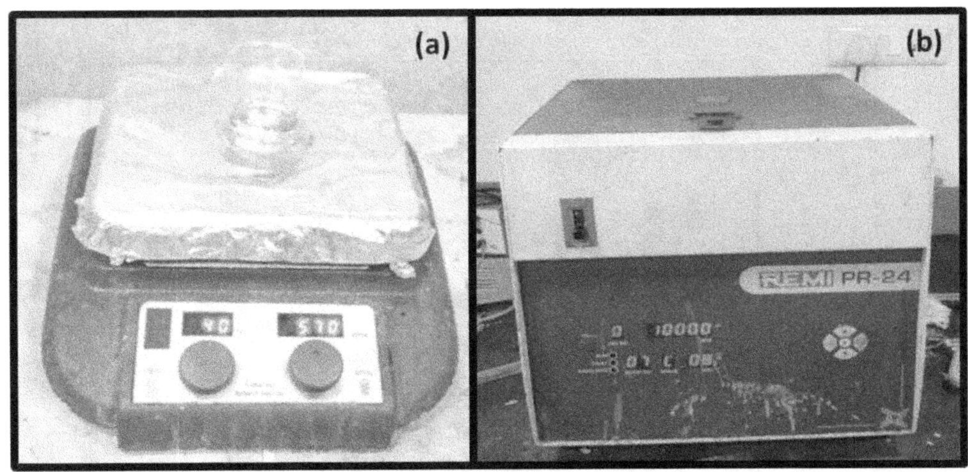

Figure.3.3 Photographs of the (a) magnetic stirrer and (b) Centrifuge.

3.3. Principle and Description of Characterizing Instruments

To characterize the samples several sophisticate instruments were used. A brief description of all those instruments and their working principal are given in the following section.

3.3.1 X-Ray Diffractometer (XRD)

The structural properties of the prepared materials can investigate by well-known X-ray diffraction method. This technique has been applied to stress and strain measurement, chemical phase analysis, the study of phase equilibrium, measurement of particle size, as well as to determine crystal structure. A Rigaku-Ultima III X-ray diffractometer with CuKα radiation (λ = 1.5418 Å) was used for characterization of the synthesized samples. When a highly collimated beam of X-rays fall on a material, due to the diffraction from the crystalline phases of the sample a diffraction pattern is observe. To determine the materials and its structural properties, the obtained diffraction patterned is used. One can easily found the lattice spacing from this diffraction pattern using 1st order Bragg's equation.

$$\lambda = 2d \sin\theta$$

Where λ = wavelength of electron,

 d = Interplanar spacing and

 θ = glancing angle.

In terms of the angle of diffraction 2θ and orientation of the sample, diffracted X-rays intensity is measured. Fig.3.4 shows schematic diagram of the X-Ray Diffractometer (XRD).

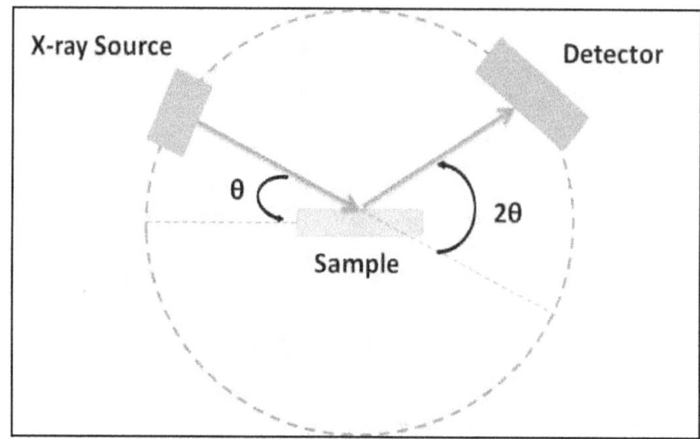

Figure.3.4 Schematic diagram of the X-Ray Diffractometer (XRD)

3.3.2. Ultraviolet-visible-near infrared (UV-Vis-NIR) spectrophotometer

UV-Vis spectroscopy (Lambda-950 spectrometer, Perkin Elmer, USA) spectrophotometer was used to measure the extent to which the sample absorb or transmit the light of varying wavelength. The wavelength could be varied from 200 to 3500 nm. Also reflectance globe was attached to the instrument for recording the reflectance of the sample. Figure 3.5 shows Block diagram of UV-Vis-NIR spectrophotometer.

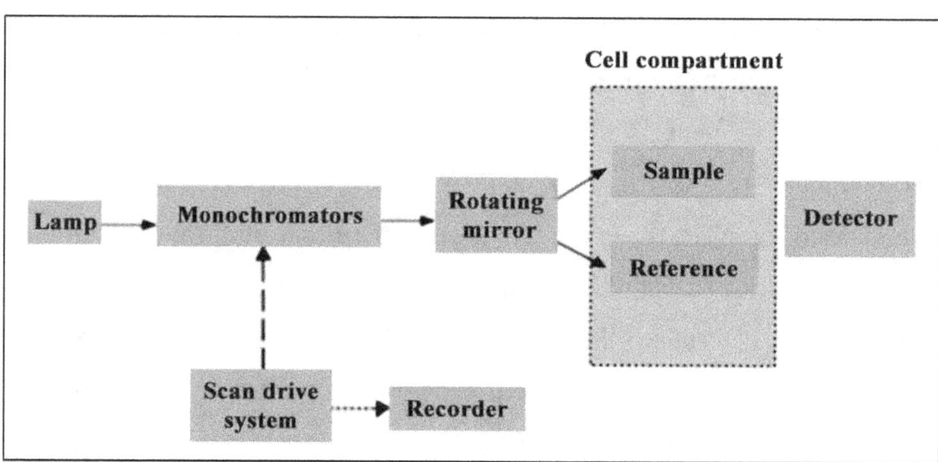

Figure.3.5 Schematic diagram of the Ultraviolet-visible-near infrared (UV-Vis-NIR) spectrophotometer

3.3.3. X-ray photoelectron spectrometer

X-ray photoelectron spectroscopy (ULVAC-PHI5000 Versa Probe II spectrometer) with Al Kα radiation source of photon energy 1486.6 eV was used to examine the composition of the material of samples and chemical state of the dopants of the sample.

39

Fig.3.6 represent the schematically diagram of (mechanism) electron emission from metal surface. X-ray of known energy falls on a material due to which photoemission of electron from the sample takes place. Relation between kinetic energy (E_k) of the emitted electron and the binding energy (E_b) is $E_b=h\nu-E_k$, where $h\nu$ is the energy of incident X-Ray, which can be measured as a function of number of electrons through the instrument. Every element has its own set of binding energies because of that unique property; XPS can be used to recognize the surface element of the samples. The concentration of the elements can also be determined by the Peak areas at nominal binding energies.

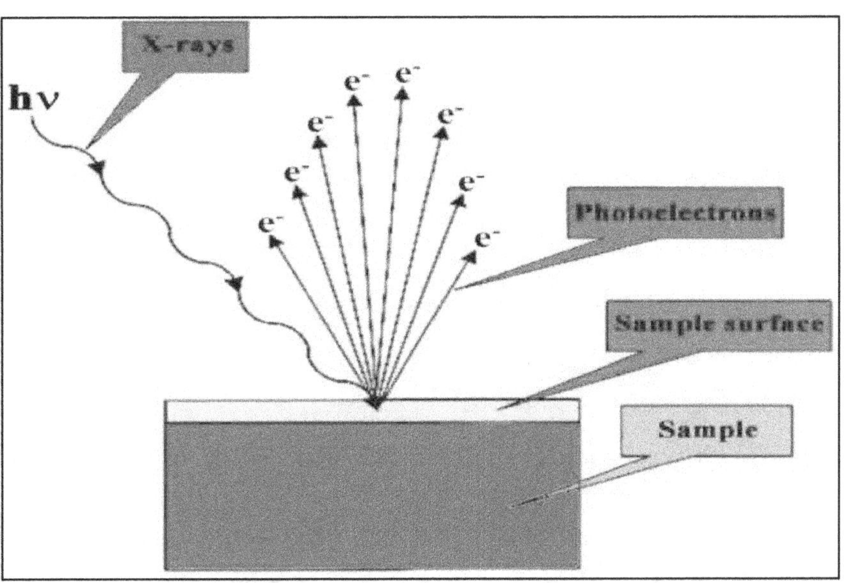

Figure.3.6 Schematic diagram of the X-ray photoelectron spectrometer.

3.3.5 Field Emission Scanning Electron Microscope (FESEM)

Field emission scanning electron microscope (FESEM) images were taken by a FEI; MERLIN (Carl Zeiss) and SUPRA40 field emission scanning electron microscope.Surface morphology of the samples was determined by FESEM images. The resolution of the instrument was 3 nm. The accelerating voltage is lying in the range between 1.5 to 30 kV, in 55 steps. The magnification could be varied 12 to 10^6 X. Probe-current range was 4 pA -10 nA. The schematic diagram of the scanning electron microscope is shown in Fig.3.7

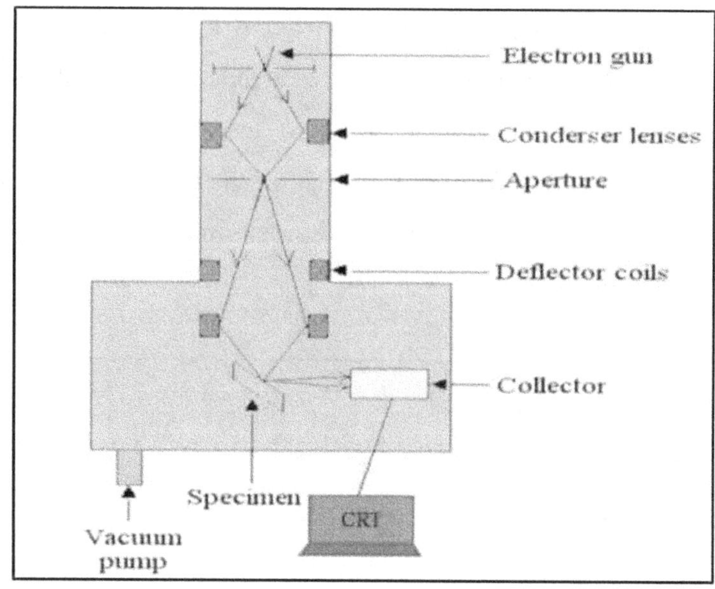

Figure.3.7 Schematic diagram of the Scanning Electron Microscope (SEM) and Field Emission Scanning.

3.3.4. High-resolution Transmission Electron Microscope (HRTEM)

A beam of electrons is spread through several apertures and lenses in the HRTEM setup. The image is focused on a phosphor screen after passed the beams through the samples. The beam may pass through the sample because the electron beam is much more energetic than the beam used in SEM (150-250 kV in HRTEM compared to 1.5-30 kV in FESEM). So, the samples with lesser thickness (< 100 nm) can give good quality images in HRTEM than in SEM. The advantages of HRTEM are high resolution, easy particle size measurement and the ability to determine crystallinity easily. This means that very small crystals can be identified and their crystal structures can be determined easily. A useful crystallographic data can also be obtained from selected area electron diffraction pattern. A schematic diagram of HRTEM is shown in Fig.3.8. In this work a transmission electron microscope (JEM 2100, at an accelerating voltage of 200 keV) was used to study the microstructure of the various samples.

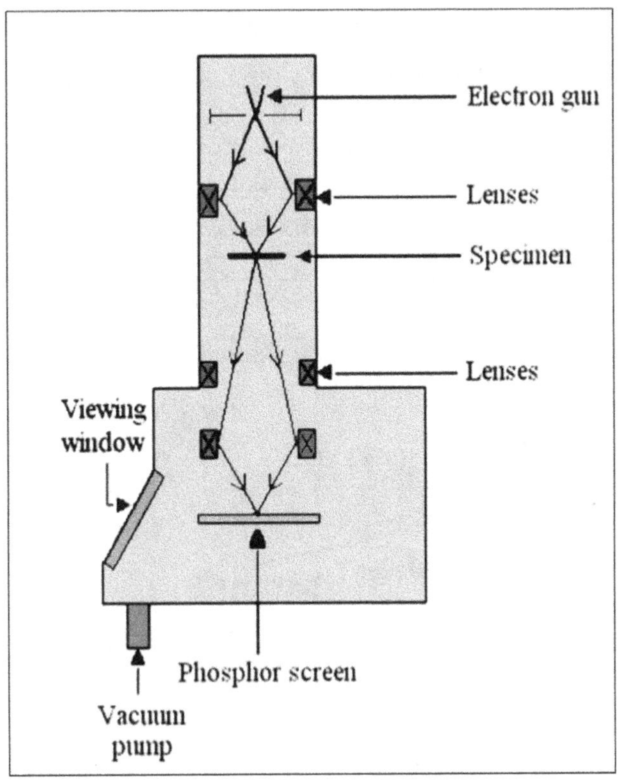

Figure.3.8 Schematic diagram of the High-resolution Transmission Electron Microscope (HRTEM)

3.3.5. Atomic Force Microscope (AFM)

Atomic Force Microscopy (VEECO di CP-II AFM), was used to study the morphology of the thin films. Due to superior resolution, the AFM has some advantages over (SEM). The AFM provides direct height measurements, extraordinary topographic contrast, and unobscured views of surface features. In addition there is no coating required for AFM measurements.

In AFM without expensive sample preparation, 3-dimensional AFM images are obtained and more complete information than the 2-dimensional profiles available from cross-sectioned samples. In general the force acting between the cantilever and the sample is a sum of Vander Waals, electrostatic, magnetic, electro-dynamic and capillary forces, which are compensated by elasticity forces resulting from the cantilever bending and the sample deformation. Cantilevers are normally 100 to 350 microns long, 0.3 to 2 microns thick and their width is about 40 microns. Thick and short cantilevers, as a rule, have high spring constant and differ in higher resonant frequencies. The cantilevers spring constants are within the range from 10^{-2} up to 10^{2} N/m. This allows using appropriate probes both for soft samples study, for example, biological objects, and for performing the AFM lithography (nano scratching).A simple schematic diagram of the AFM is shown in the Figure 3.9.

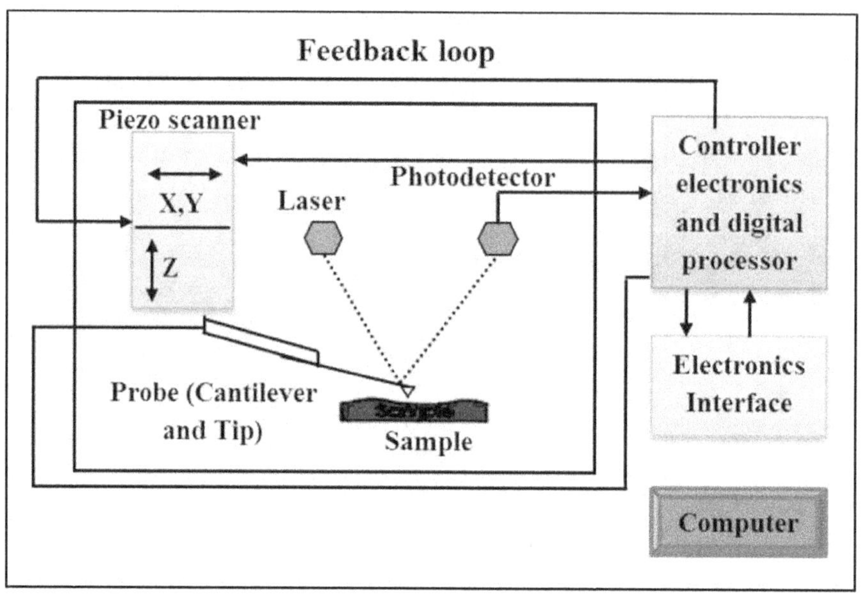

Figure.3.9 Schematic diagram of the Atomic Force Microscope (AFM)

3.3.6. Raman spectroscopy

To study the vibrational properties of the nanostructured material, Raman spectroscopy is one of the useful tools. From the Raman Spectroscopy, the information about structure, phase, phonon confinement, grain size etc. can be determined. When a monochromatic radiation is scattered by molecules, a small fraction of the scattered radiation is observed to have a different frequency from the incident one due to the inelastic scattering. This down converted frequency shift is known as Strokes shifted scattering. Whereas, when the incident radiation absorbs a phonon and emerges with higher energy Anti-strokes shift scattering occurs. A stroke mode scattering is usually monitored because Anti-strokes mode is weaker than the Stroked mode.In Raman Spectroscopy, an intense monochromatic radiation, i.e., a laser source is incident on the sample. The weak scattered light is passed through the monochromator to reject the Raleigh scattering and Photodetector detect the Raman shifted wavelength. The phonon confinement in a material can be observed as the shift in the Raman line frequencies from the bulk material. Acoustic modes of bulk materials are not observable because of their low frequencies but in case of nanostructured material it appears in the measurable range. The frequency of the acoustic mode is inversely proportional to the size of the particles. Confinement of optical phonon results in the frequency shift and asymmetrical broadening of longitudinal (LO) and transverse optical (TO) mode line shape. In the present work, Raman spectra were obtained with Raman spectroscopy (IHR550 and the laser of excitation wavelength 532 nm).The picture of the block diagram of the optical instrument is shown in Fig. 3.10.

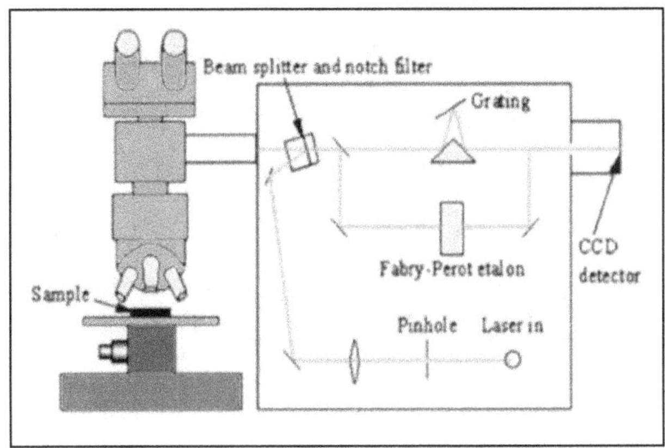

Figure.3.10 Schematic diagram of the Raman spectroscopy

3.4 Experimental techniques for studying electrochemical performances of supercapacitors

In the present study we have done cyclic voltammetry, galvanometric charging discharging and electrochemical impedance spectroscopy to investigate the performance of supercapacitors using CHI 600E Series Electrochemical Analyzer/Workstation as shown in the fig 3.11.

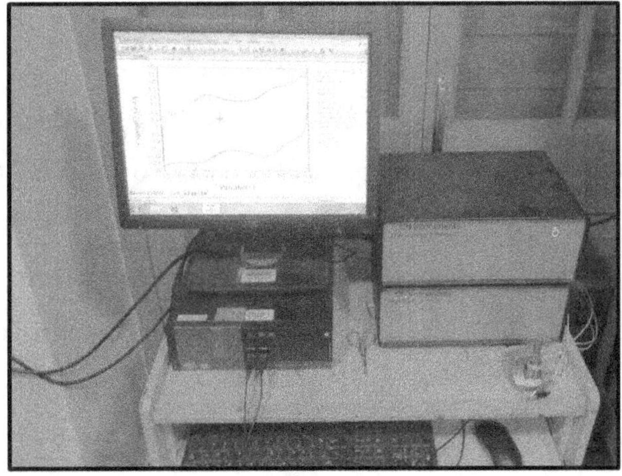

Figure.3.11 CHI 600E Series Electrochemical Analyzer/Workstation.

A brief description of the methods employed is given below:

(a) Cyclic voltammetry:

Cyclic voltammetry is a well-known technique to study the electrochemical performance of supercapacitors, in which a potential is applied to the working electrodes at a constant rate and current flowing through the electrode is measured over a specified potential window. EDLCs shows rectangular shaped CV curves whereas PSCs shows redox peaks in their CV curves.

The specific capacitance of the two electrode symmetric and asymmetric supercapacitors can be calculated from the CV curves using equations (1) and (2) respectively, where m is the total mass of the electrode materials, v (V/s) is the scan rate and ΔV represent potential window. Energy density (E) and power density (P) can also be calculated from the equations (3) and (4) for symmetric supercapacitor and that for asymmetric supercapacitor from equations (5) and (6).[1-3]

$$C_{symmetric} = \frac{4 \int I_1 \, dV}{vm\Delta V} \, ...(1)$$

$$C_{asymmetric} = \frac{2 \int I_1 \, dV}{vm\Delta V} \, ...(2)$$

$$E_{symmetric} = \frac{1}{8} C(\Delta V)^2 \, ...\quad(3)$$

$$P_{symmetric} = \frac{1}{8} C \, \Delta V v \quad ....(4)$$

$$E_{asymmetric} = \frac{1}{4} C(\Delta V)^2 \, ...\quad(5)$$

$$P_{asymmetric} = \frac{1}{4} C \, \Delta V v \quad ....(6)$$

(b) Galvanometric charging discharging (GCD):

In GCD measurements a constant current density is applied between the electrodes until the lower or higher potential is reached. We can also calculate the specific capacitances from the GCD curves according to the equations (7) and (8) for symmetric and asymmetric two electrode supercapacitors respectively, where m is the total mass of the electrode materials, I is the applied current and $\Delta V/\Delta t$ represent slope of the discharge curves after IR drop. [45] The internal resistance of the supercapacitors can also be calculated from the very short IR drop, which is obtained in the initial portion of the discharge curves. For EDLC rest of the discharge curve after IR drop is linear and that for PSCs and HSCs large deviations in linearity occurs.

$$C_{symmetric} = \frac{4I\,\Delta t}{m\,\Delta V} \quad \ldots\ldots\ldots\ldots\ldots (7)$$

$$C_{asymmetric} = \frac{2I\,\Delta t}{m\Delta V} \quad \ldots\ldots\ldots\ldots\ldots (8)$$

(c) Electrochemical impedance spectroscopy (EIS):

Kinetic parameters of the electrochemical processes such as charge transfer, ion diffusion can easily determine by the electrochemical impedance spectroscopy technique, where the impedance data are recorded at the open circuit voltage by applying a small alternating voltage ($\pm$ 5mV to $\pm$10 mV) over a frequency window (1mHz to 1MHz).The series resistance (R_s) and charge transfer resistance (R_{ct}) can be calculated from the EIS graph (Nyquist plot).The diameter of the semicircle in the medium frequency region represent the value of R_{ct}, Low value of R_{ct} indicates fast electrochemical reactions. An inclined line a in the low frequency region displays Warburg impedance. From the linear part of the Bode plot (log |Z| vs. log n curve) capacitance value can also be calculated from the equation (9), where |Z| and n represent the imaginary part of impedance and frequency respectively. [4] The Bode plots show that capacitance value decreases with the increasing frequency because at high frequency electrolyte ions cannot penetrate into the microspores.

$$C = \frac{1}{2\pi f|Z|} \quad \ldots\ldots\ldots\ldots\ldots (9)$$

3.5 References

1. C. Wu, X. Lu, L. Peng, K. Xu, X. Peng, J. Huang, G. Yu and Y. Xie, Nat.Commun., 2013, 4, 2431.

2. H. Wang, H. Yi, X Chen and X. Wang, J. Mater. Chem. A 2014, 2, 3223-3230.

3. S. Ratha and C. S. Rout. RSC Adv. 2015, 5, 86551-86557.

4. P. Taberna, P. Simon and J.F. Fauvarque, Journal of the Electrochemical Society, 2003, 150, A292-A300.

Chapter4

Large Scale Production of Transition Metal Oxides Nano Sheets by Mixed Solvent Exfoliation for Supercapacitor Application

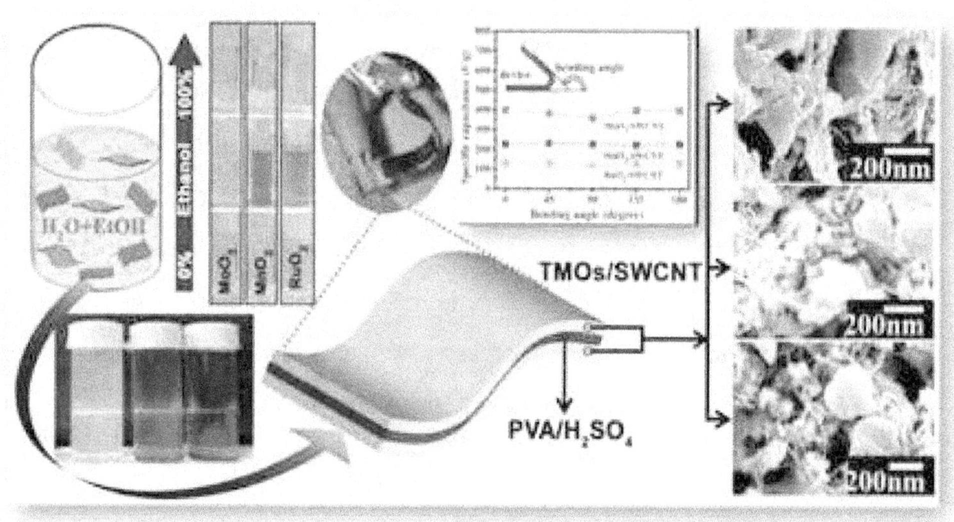

Work presented in this chapter has been published in:

(1)New J. Chem., 2019, 43, 12385-12395

<u>Shibsankar Dutta</u>, Shreyasi Pal, Sukanta De

(2) AIP Conf. Proc., 2018, 1953, 030145

<u>Shibsankar Dutta</u>, Shreyasi Pal and Sukanta De

4.1. Introduction

This chapter enlightens a simple mixed solvent assisted ultrasonic method to exfoliate transition metal oxides (TMOs) nano sheets using the proper composition of ethanol and water. These well dispersed stable solutions were used to make thin film of TMOs nanosheets which can be readily transferred on wide range of substrates for different applications. TMOs/SWCNT based solid state flexible supercapacitors demonstrated enhanced electrochemical performance.

A number of nanostructured pseudocapacitive materials including transition metal oxides (TMO), [1-9] transition metal dichalcogenides [10], hydroxides[11-13] and conductive polymer materials[14-18] have been used for supercapacitor applications. Among them 2-D graphene analogues (GA) are the best choices for the highly flexible ultrathin-film supercapacitor.[10,11,19] 2-D nanomaterials provides remarkable prospects for both fundamental studies and several technological applications due to their unique and intriguing properties,[20-24] Therefore, the large scale production of 2-D pseudocapacitive materials is much needed for constructing high performance flexible supercapacitors.

In their 2-D structure, inorganic layered materials such as transition metal oxides (MnO_2, RuO_2, MoO_3, TiO_2 etc) and transition metal dichalcogenides (MoS_2, WS_2, VS_2, etc) for their unique properties becomes promising candidates for topological insulators, energy harvesters, thermal conductors, and transistors.[1-9,25-30] Among them transition metal oxides play importance roles to develop environment friendly energy storage devices in the form of pseudocapacitors.[31-34]To exploit their full potential layered materials must be exfoliated. Liquid phase exfoliation of layered materials is most appropriate technique to produce 2-D nanomaterials for many practical applications, especially for thin film formation.[35-41] Depending on the materials, certain solvents [36,38,40-44] or solvent blends,[45] aqueous surfactant solutions,[35,39,46] or polymer solutions[47,48] can be used as stabilizing liquids. For application in supercapacitor electrodes, liquid suspended 2-D nanomaterials or their composite needs to process into films. Liquid phase exfoliated 2-D TMOs and their composites with carbonaceous materials could be suitable to develop thin film flexible electrodes for application in supercapacitors due to excellent electrochemical properties that come from rich selection of atomic types in the 2D lattice plane. Non-volatile high boiling point organic solvents are suitable for liquid exfoliation according to the thermodynamics study, but non-volatile solvents are difficult to remove after film formation, which provides us the limitations of their use in practical device applications. [39,40,49] Also complete removal of surfactants or polymers from thin films prepared from aqueous surfactant solutions or polymer solutions suspended 2-D nanomaterials is very difficult. The water base mixed solvent is not only suitable to remove easily; they are much less toxic compare to other organic solvents such as NMP, DMF, iso-propanol, chloroform, acetone, DMSO etc. If we can achieve to exfoliate layered transition metal oxides in to their 2-D nanosheets in large scale in water base mix solvents, could be useful to fabricate eco-friendly devices with high performance.

4.2. Experimental section

All the chemicals, Molybdenum Trioxide (MoO_3) (99.5%), Manganese (IV) Oxide (MnO_2) (≥90%), Ruthenium (IV) Oxide (RuO_2) (99.9%) were bought from Sigma-Aldrich. Ethanol and deionized water (D.I.) involved in this work were bought from Merck. Three different transition metal oxides (MoO_3, RuO_2, and MnO_2) were dispersed in different vol% ethanol/water mixture with an initial concentration 20 mg/ml using high power tip sonicator for 30 minutes followed by bath sonicator for 6 hours. Subsequently, they were centrifuged at 1500 rpm for 90 minutes. The supernatants having high concentrations of 2D TMOs flakes were decanted and subjected to further characterization. The Schematic diagram of the mixed solvent exfoliation of the 2-D materials is shown in the fig. 4.1.

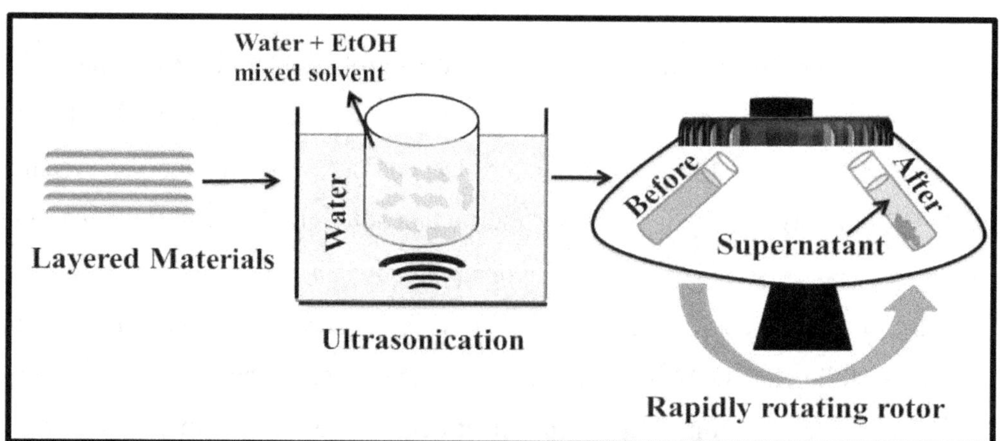

Figure 4.1 Schematic diagram of the mixed solvent exfoliation of the 2-D materials.

4.3. Thin Films Preparation and Device Fabrication

4.3.1. Symmetric flexible supercapacitor fabrication

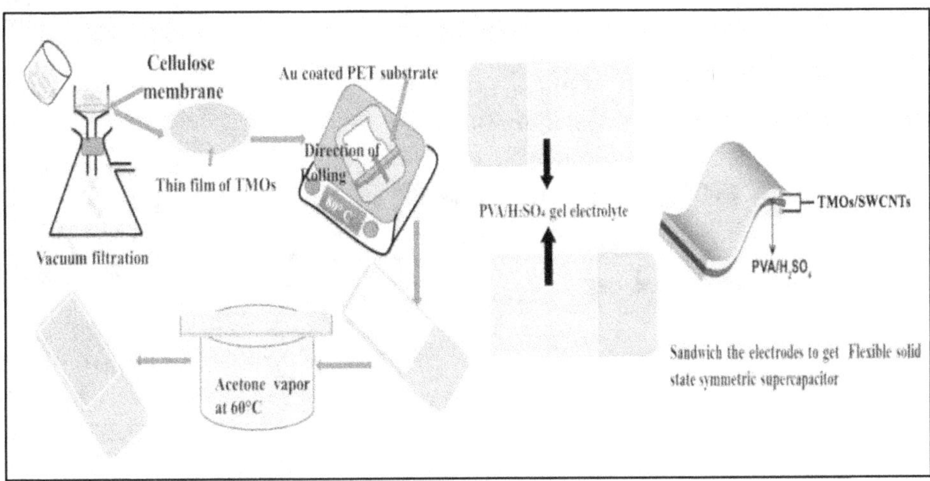

Figure 4.2 Schematic diagrams of Thin Films Preparation and Device Fabrication.

The dispersion of TMOs nanosheets prepared in this method allowed us to make thin films of TMOs nanosheets and their composites with carbonaceous nanostructure by vacuum filtration with thickness ranging from a few nanometers to micrometers. The thin films were then transferred onto a flexible gold coated PET substrate by acetone vapor and acetone bath treatments for device fabrication. Fig.4.2 represents the thin films and device fabrication technique.

4.3.2. In-plane supercapacitor device fabrication

In planner supercapacitors, requirement of a separator is eliminated because the electrolyte ions are transported two-dimensionally. Here we present a mixed solvent exfoliation of MnO_2 nanosheets for high performance planer supercapacitors. In particular, the planar structures supercapacitors constructed by MnO_2 nanosheets integrated with SWCNT. Schematic 4.3 represent the in-plane device fabrication technique.

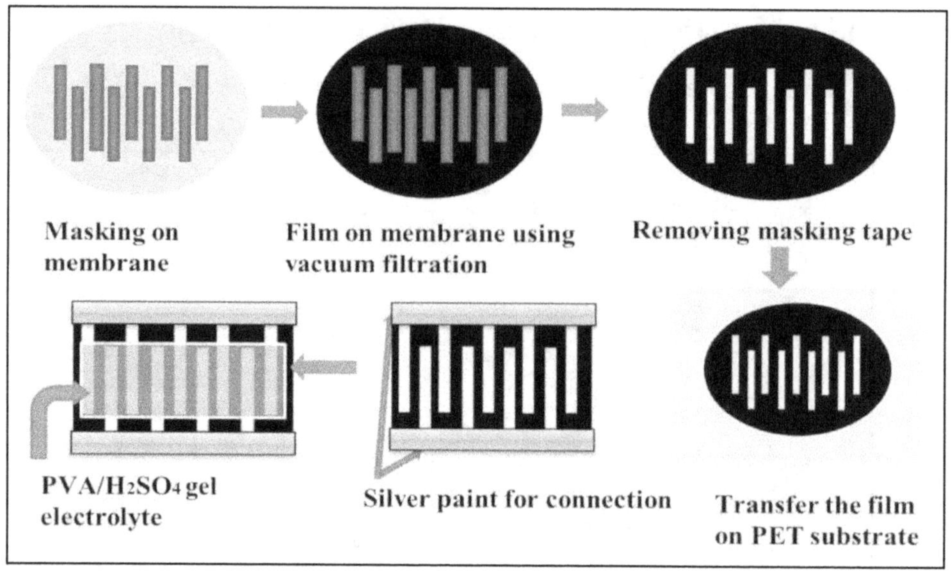

Figure 4.3 Schematic diagrams of In-plane supercapacitor fabrication.

4.4. Materials Characterization

The as-synthesized samples were characterized using UV-Vis spectroscopy (Lambda-950 spectrometer, Perkin Elmer, USA), Raman spectroscopy (IHR550 and the laser of excitation wavelength 532 nm), transmission electron microscope (TEM, JEM-2010), field emission scanning electron microscope (FESEM HITACHI S-4800), atomic force microscopy (VEECO di CP-II AFM), X-ray photoelectron spectroscopy (ULVAC-PHI5000 Versa Probe II spectrometer) with Al Kα radiation source of photon energy 1486.6 eV. BET analyses of the samples were studied using Autosorb iQ Station 1 instrument using liquid nitrogen at 77 K. All Electrochemical measurements were done using CHI 660E.

4.5. Results and discussion

4.5.1. Exfoliation of TMOs:

To explore the possibilities of liquid phase exfoliation of Transition metal oxides (TMOs) in mixture of two low boiling point and volatile solvents, we have sonicated as received TMOs (MoO_3, MnO_2 and RuO_2) with initial concentration (C_i) 20 mg/ml in mixed solvents of water and ethanol with different volume fractions and centrifuge to get rid of un-exfoliated oxide materials. Digital images of suspensions containing exfoliated MoO_3, MnO_2 and RuO_2 in different ethanol/water mixtures in inset of Figure 4.4 (a-c), shows that the concentration of suspension is varying with ethanol/water ratio. To analyze quantitatively, we have recorded absorption spectra for all dispersions and took the measured of absorbance per unit cell length (A/l) at 375 nm, 380 nm and 450 nm for MoO$_3$, MnO$_2$ and RuO$_2$ respectively which can be used as metric to determine the concentration of TMOs in dispersion. The variation of A/l with volume fraction of ethanol in water (Figure 4.4 (a-c)) clearly shows that pure ethanol or pure water hardly can disperse oxide materials but the concentrations of TMOs dispersions are directly dependent on the volume fraction of ethanol in water with peak at 65% ethanol in water for MoO$_3$. Whereas for both MnO$_2$ and RuO$_2$ peak value of A/l is at 50% mixed solvent.

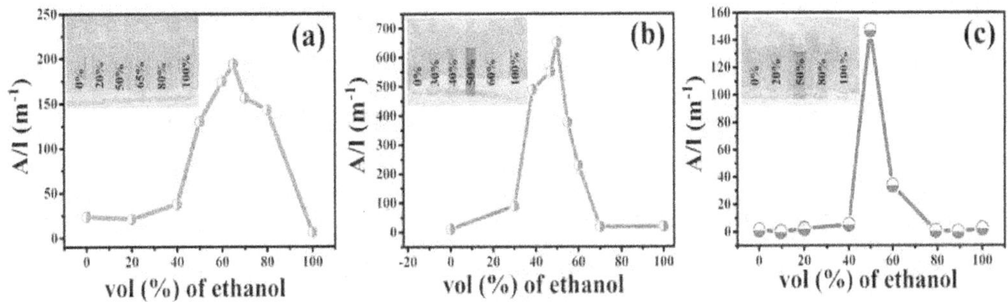

Figure 4.4. (a-c) Graph of A/l vs volume fraction (ethanol) in water for the MoO$_3$, MnO$_2$ and RuO$_2$ nanosheets respectively; Inset showing their corresponding digital images of different vol% EtOH

The dissolution behavior can be explained by the Hansen solubility parameter (HSP) [50-51] theory based on the three solubility parameters, these three dispersive (δ_D), polar (δ_P) and hydrogen bonding (δ_H) solubility parameters of solvent and solute are interrelated by the equation 1.

$$R_a = [4(\delta_{Dsolv} - \delta_{Dsolu})^2 + (\delta_{Psolv} - \delta_{Psolu})^2 + (\delta_{Hsolv} - \delta_{Hsolu})^2]^{\frac{1}{2}} \quad (1)$$

The solubility directly depends on the HSP distance (R$_a$) value, smaller R$_a$ value provides us higher solubility.

Mixed solvent exfoliation can also be explained by Hansen theory where the each of three parameters is linear function of the volume fraction of the composition [equation 2].

$$\delta_{blend} = \sum \phi_{n,comp} \delta_{n,comp} \quad (2)$$

Where ϕ defines the volume fraction of each composition. Based on these two equations different solvent mixture can be predicted for the nanomaterial's exfoliation.

Initially the dispersed concentration can be measured by filtering an appropriate amount of the dispersion and weighing the deposited film. A sample of stock dispersion was then serially diluted with solvent (65% ethanol in water for MoO_3 and 50% ethanol in water for MnO_2 and RuO_2) and measured the absorbance. A straight line fit of absorbance per unit length (A/l) Vs concentration (after centrifuge) as shown in Figure 4.5(a-c), gives the accurate value of absorption coefficient (α). Measured α (at 375 nm) for MoO_3 is 596 mg^{-1} ml m^{-1} and is in reasonable agreement with the previously reported value [41] (note: we have calculated from their reported A/l and concentration value to compare), gives the concentration of dispersed MoO_3 to be 0.33 mg/ml. Most interestingly this is almost 3 times higher than that of in IPA, [41] even the initial concentration was 15 times lower in our case. Absorption coefficient for MnO_2 (at 380 nm) and RuO_2 (at 450 nm) were measured to be 2937 mg^{-1} ml m^{-1} and 641 mg^{-1} ml m^{-1} respectively. The obtained concentration of the dispersed MnO_2 and RuO_2 (C_i=20 mg/ml) was 0.22 mg/ml and 0.23 mg/ml respectively.

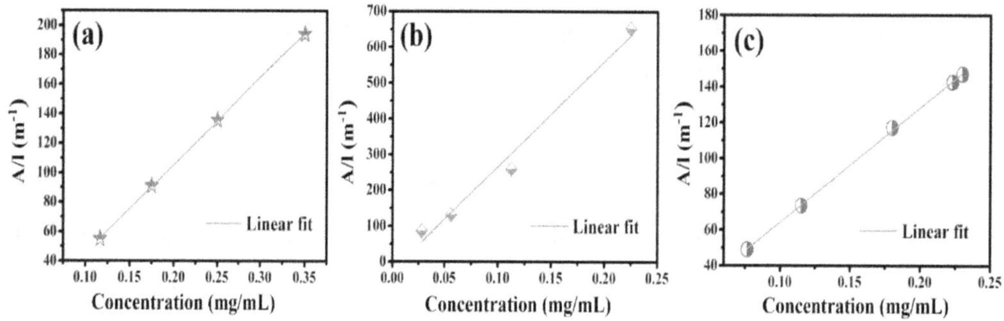

Figure 4.5. Absorbance per unit length (A/l) vs concentration (a) MoO_3, (b) MnO_2, (c) RuO_2.

Maximize the dispersed concentration is very much required for applications and previous report shows that initial concentration plays an important role in it. To address this, with the knowledge of different parameters including the composition of mixed solvents for the stable dispersion we have prepared dispersions for a range of initial concentration (C_i) of oxide materials. We have plotted absorbance per unit length (A/l) vs C_i shown in Figure 4.6(a-c), observing a linear increase in dispersed concentration for all three oxides upto C_i = 60mg/ml after which saturation of solute in solvents is approached.

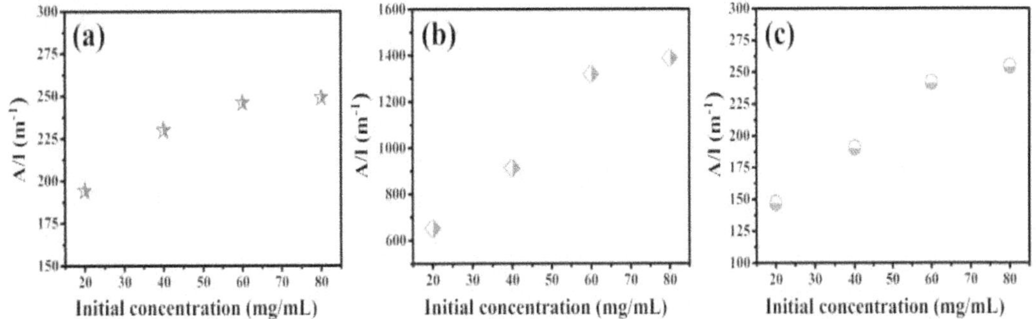

Figure 4.6. Absorbance per unit length (A/l) vs initial concentration (a) MoO_3, (b) MnO_2, (c) RuO_2.

The final concentrations of dispersions were obtained 0.42 mg/ml, 0.47 mg/ml and 0.40 mg/ml for MoO_3, MnO_2 and RuO_2 respectively. The dispersed concentrations of exfoliated TMOs are much higher than the previously reported data's.[41, 52] The TMOs nanosheets were well dispersed in ethanol/water mixed solution showing the Tyndall effect (Figure 4.7).

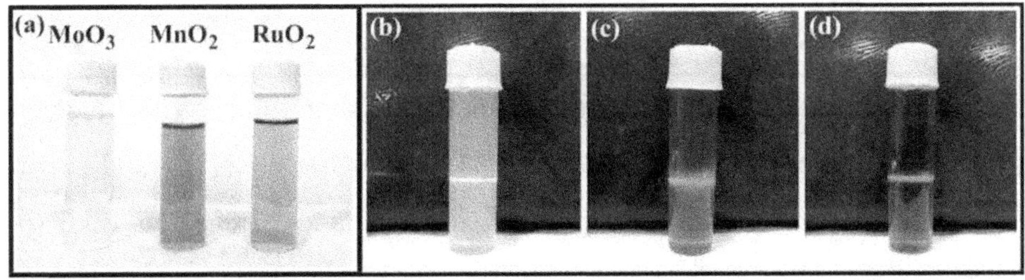

Figure 4.7. (a) Digital images of the MoO_3, MnO_2 and RuO_2 nanosheets dispersion in Ethanol/ water, (b-d) Tyndall effect of the exfoliated MoO_3, MnO_2 and RuO_2 nanosheets respectively.

Figure 4.8. MoO$_3$, MnO$_2$ and RuO$_2$ nanosheets thin films on (a-c) glass, (d-f) PET substrate respectively. MoO$_3$/SWCNT, MnO$_2$/SWCNT and RuO$_2$/SWCNT nanocomposites thin films on (g-i) Si substrate and Au coated PET (j-l) substrate respectively

Once we have stable dispersions, thin films of bare TMOs can be prepared by vacuum filtration[41] with thickness ranging from few nanometers to few hundreds of micrometer on cellulose membrane. These thin films can be deposited on suitable substrate as required for device applications. We have shown our films can be transfer on different substrates as shown in the Figure 4.8.

4.5.2 Structural and morphological characterization

The atomic force microscopy (AFM) images shown in Figure 4.9(a-c) of the metal oxides clearly revealed the presence of nanosheets of the metal oxides with an average thickness of 1.85 nm for MoO$_3$, 1.07 nm for MnO$_2$ and 2.1 nm for RuO$_2$ respectively, denoting that our exfoliated metal oxides are mostly bi-layers.[53-55]

For detail structural and morphology study, TEM analysis was performed on exfoliated TMOs by depositing few drops of each dispersion onto TEM grids. In all cases, a large numbers of quasi-2D nanosheets were seen, with typical example as shown in Figure 4.10(a-c). Figure 4.10a represents the TEM image of MoO_3 nanosheet with lateral dimension of ~300 nm to 400 nm. We also studied HRTEM imaging of exfoliated MoO_3, which clearly shows the crystalline structure as displays in the Figure 4.10d. The measured interplanar spacing of MoO_3 nanosheet is 0.39 nm and 0.37 nm, corresponds to the typical interplanar spacing of the (100) and (001) respectively.[56,57] Low magnification TEM image in the Figure 4.10b displays the sheet like morphology of MnO_2 with lateral dimension ~300 nm. High resolution TEM (HRTEM) images of the nanosheets in Figure 4.10e clearly shows that MnO_2 nanosheets were crystallized with the interplanar distance of 0.253 nm corresponding to the (200) plane.[58-60] 2-D nanosheet of RuO_2 have lateral dimension also of ~100 nm measured from TEM image as shown in the Figure 4.10c and lattice spacing of 0.237 nm corresponds to the (110) plane, clearly shown in the HRTEM image displayed in Figure 4.10f.[61-63] Further the SAED patterns of all TMOs (insets of Figure 4.10(d-f)) indicate their single crystalline nature. Lateral dimension of TMOs nanosheets measured from low resolution TEM images are in good agreement with the dimension of nanosheets in AFM images.

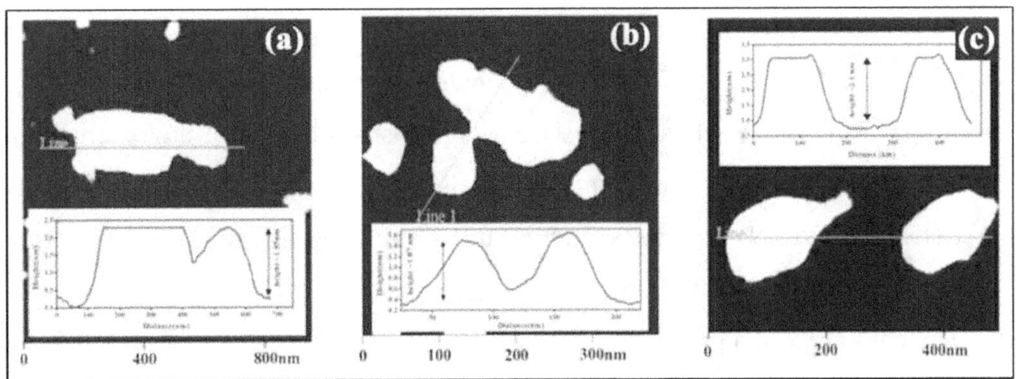

Figure 4.9. Atomic force microscopy (AFM) analysis of (a) MoO_3, (b) MnO_2 and (c) RuO_2 nanosheets respectively

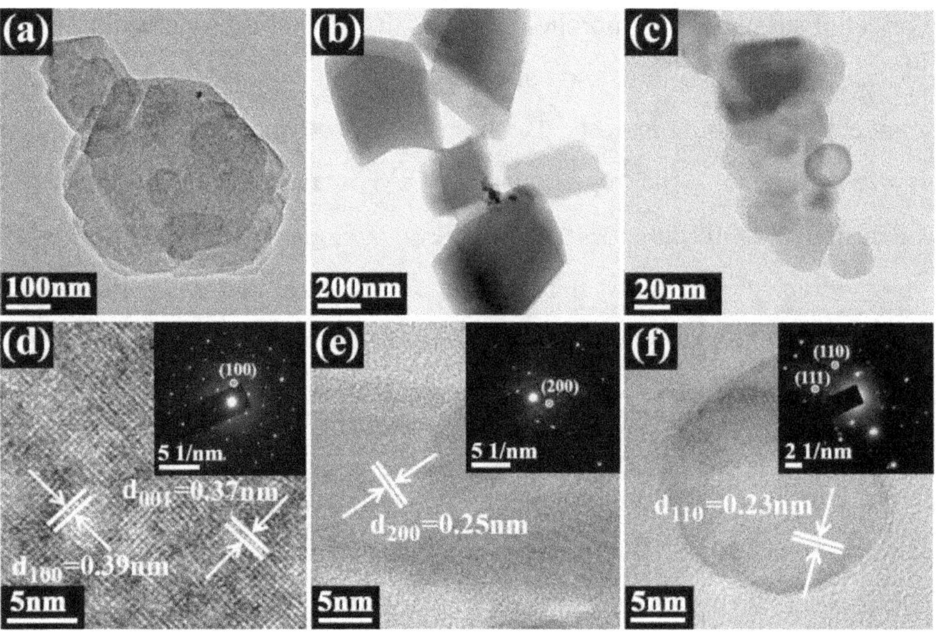

Figure4.10. (a-c) Transmission electron microscopy (TEM) images and (d-f) high-resolution TEM analysis with selected area electron diffraction (SAED) pattern in the inset of MoO_3, MnO_2 and RuO_2 respectively.

Figure 4.11 (a-c) displays the Raman spectra of the exfoliated metal oxide thin films. Three main peaks at 671, 827 and 965 cm^{-1} in the Figure 4.11a were observed for the MoO_3.[53] The 671 cm^{-1} peak is assigned to the stretching mode of triply coordinated oxygen (Mo_3–O) which arises from edge-shared oxygen atoms in common to three octahedral. The peak at 827 cm^{-1} is attributed to the doubly coordinated oxygen (Mo_2–O) stretching mode which results from corner-sharing oxygen atoms common to two octahedral.[64] Finally, the peak at 995 cm^{-1} is assigned to the terminal oxygen (Mo^{6+}=O) stretching mode which results from an unshared oxygen. The Raman spectrum of thin film of exfoliated MnO_2 in Figure 4.11b shows peaks at 510, 575, and 642 cm^{-1}, almost identical as reported previously.[65] The peak at 642 cm^{-1} corresponding to the symmetric stretching vibration v_2 (Mn–O) of MnO_6 groups. Whereas the band located at 575 cm^{-1} is due to the v_3 (Mn–O) stretching vibration in the basal plane of [MnO_6] sheets. The three major Raman features located at 528, 644 and 716 cm^{-1} of RuO_2 presented in the Figure 4.11c correspond to E_g, A_{1g} and B_{2g} modes respectively.[66]

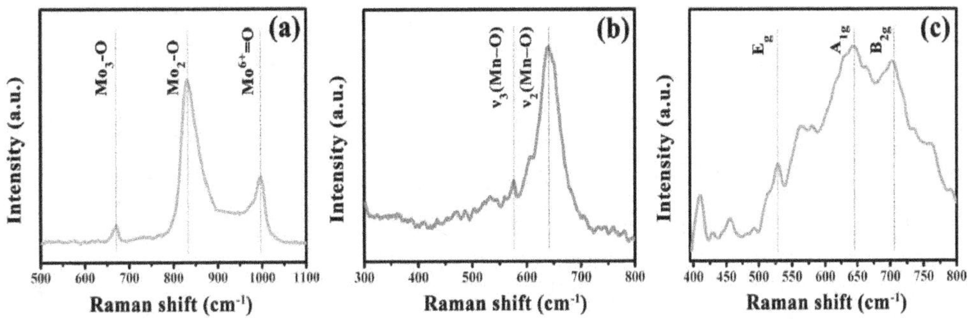

Figure 4.11. Raman Spectra of MoO_3 (a), MnO_2 (b) RuO_2(c) nanosheets thin films on silicon

Figure4.12. (a,b,c) FESEM images of the bulk MoO_3, MnO_2, RuO_2; (d,e,f) showing their high magnification FESEM images respectively.

Figure 4.12 shows FESEM images of bulk TMOs, which indicates that bulk TMOs are layered structure. Figure 4.13 (a-c) displays FESEM images of the TMOs nanosheets. 2-D nanosheet of MoO_3 have lateral dimension ~200 nm to 300 nm as shown in the Figure 4.13a, whereas the average lateral dimension of MnO_2 and RuO_2 nanosheets are 250 nm and 100 nm respectively. FESEM was done on the TMOs dispersion after filtering, so it is quite difficult to get actual boundary of the TMOs to determine the flake size individually. TEM was done on exfoliated dispersions of TMOs where we get the actual size of the individual nanosheets as discuss previously. Liquid phase exfoliated stable dispersion facilitate formation of hybrids or composites of 2D nanomaterials with polymers, carbon nanostructures or other different nanomaterials.

After ultrasonic agitation of TMOs and SWCNT might be exfoliated and dispersed in ethanol/water mixer and forming a homogeneous solution of TMOs/SWCNT, which clearly shows in the FESEM images of the TMOs/SWCNT thin films on cellulose membrane [Figure 4.13(d-f)]. The as-prepared composites exhibited an interconnected porous network. In addition, the mesoporosity in the electrode serve as a path, which allow to access of electrolyte to the internal surface of the TMOs.[67]

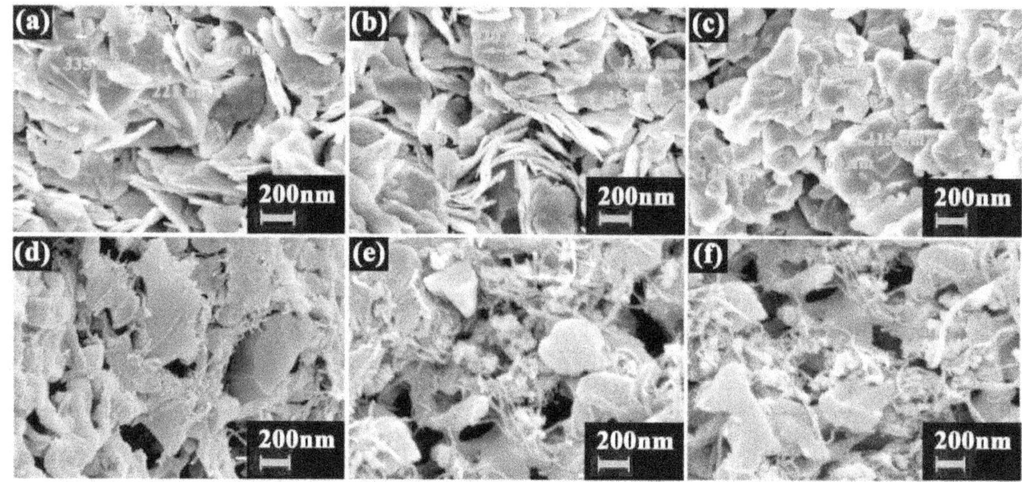

Figure 4.13 FESEM images of (a-c) metal oxide nanosheets (MoO$_3$, MnO$_2$, RuO$_2$) and (d-f) their nanocomposites (MoO$_3$/SWCNT, MnO$_2$/SWCNT, RuO$_2$/SWCNT) respectively.

To investigate the oxidation state of TMOs in the TMOs/SWCNT composites, the samples were further characterized by XPS. Figure 4.14(a,e,i) shows the XPS survey scan of three composites. No additional peak except Mo, O and C (for MoO$_3$/SWCNT), Mn, O and C (for MnO$_2$/SWCNT), and Ru, O and C (for RuO$_2$/SWCNT) was observed from the XPS survey scan. Figure 4.14b shows the Mo 3d spectrum, where two peaks located at 232.5 and 235.6 eV can be attributed to the Mo 3d$_{5/2}$ and Mo 3d$_{3/2}$ respectively, indicating 6$^+$ oxidation states for Mo.[68]

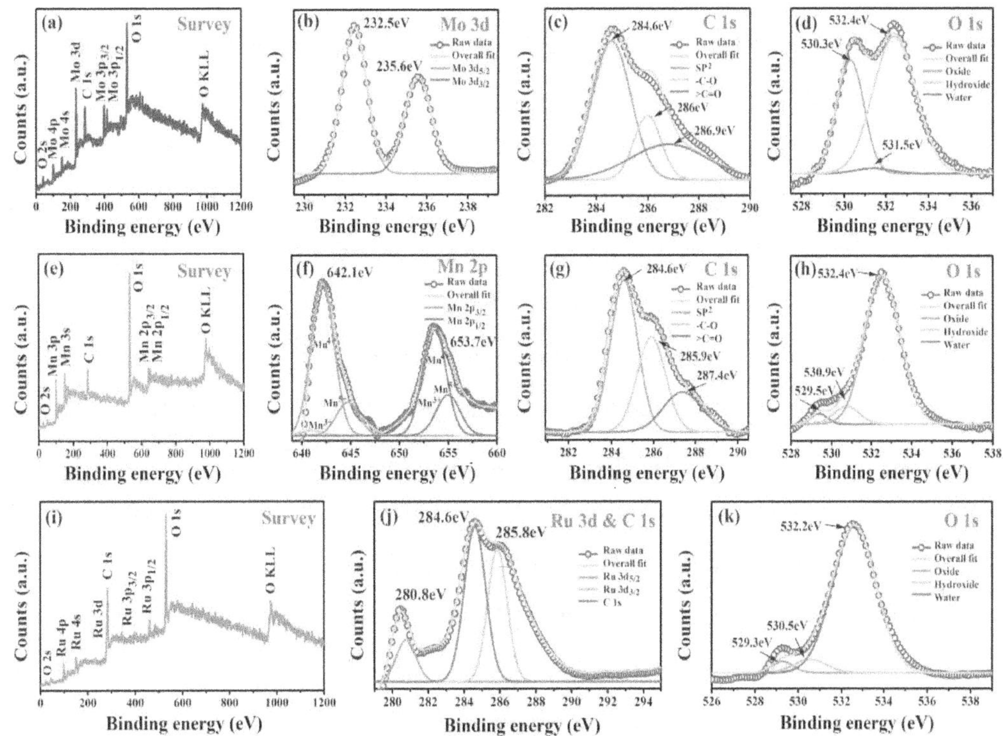

Figure 4.14. XPS spectra of MoO3/SWCNT composite: (a) survey spectrum, (b) Mo 3d, (c) C1s, (d) O1s; XPS spectra of MnO2/SWCNT composite: (e) survey spectrum, (d) Mn 2p,(c) C1s, (d) O1s: XPS spectra of RuO2/SWCNT composite: (i) survey spectrum, (j) Ru 3d, C1s and (d) O1s.

In Mn 2p spectrum multiple splitting with two main peaks can be identified at 642.1 and 653.7 eV corresponding to the excitation of Mn $2p_{3/2}$ and Mn $2p_{1/2}$ spin-orbit of Mn^{4+} in MnO_2, respectively (Figure 4.14f). The intensity of Mn^{3+} and Mn^{5+} related peaks is much weaker than that for Mn^{4+}, indicating the dominant role of Mn^{4+} in the composite.[7]The de-convoluted C 1s for MoO_3/SWCNT and MnO_2/SWCNT are shown in Figure 4.14c and Figure 4.14g respectively. The peak having binding energy 284.6 eV was assigned to the C=C bonds in CNT with SP^2 hybridization.[69] Furthermore, relatively small peaks at 286, 285.9 eV and 286.9 eV, 286.85 eV was assigned to the –C–O and >C = O functional group respectively.[70]Figure 4.14j shows the Ru 3d and C 1s spectra of the RuO_2/SWCNT nanocomposites. Two peaks of Ru 3d at 280.8 and 285.8 eV were assigned to Ru $3d_{5/2}$ and Ru $3d_{3/2}$ respectively, whereas the peak at 284.6 eV was assigned to the C=C bonds of C 1s.[3,71]The deconvoluted O 1s spectra as shown in the fig4.14(d), (h), (k) consist of three peaks at the binding energy of 530.3, 531.5 and

532.4 eV (for MoO$_3$/SWCNT), 529.5, 530.9 and 532.4 eV (for MnO$_2$/SWCNT) and 529.3, 530.5 and 532.2 eV (for RuO$_2$/SWCNT) corresponding to various oxygen-containing chemical bonds: oxide, hydroxide and water respectively.[72]

The specific surface area and porosity of the as-prepared nanocomposites have been investigated by N$_2$ adsorption and desorption measurements at 77 K. According to Brunauer-Emmett-Teller [BET] analysis, the total specific surface area of 151.4 m^2 /g, 122.8 m^2 /g, 142.6 m^2 /g were obtained for the MoO$_3$/SWCNT, MnO$_2$/SWCNT and RuO$_2$/SWCNT nanocomposites respectively (Figure 4.15c), which were much larger than that of the exfoliated metal oxides nanosheets (i.e. 55.7 m^2 /g, 48.6 m^2 /g, 53.5 m^2/ g for MoO$_3$, MnO$_2$ and RuO$_2$ nanosheets, Figure4.15a). The pore size distribution plots were obtained based on the adsorption data according to the Barrett-Joyner-Halenda (BJH) method. The D vs dV/dlogD plots for the exfoliated metal oxides (Figure 4.15b), TMOs/SWCNT composites (Figure 16d) indicates the existence of mesopores ranging from 2 to 5 nm within the nanocomposites. The total specific surface area (81.2 m^2 /g) and pore size distribution plots of the pristine SWCNT is shown in the figure 4.16(a) and (b) respectively. The large specific surface area and mesoporous structure can provide more active sites for electrochemical reactions, increase contact area and shortening ion diffusion paths between electrode and electrolyte, which are beneficial for electrolyte percolation and facilitate the ion diffusion.

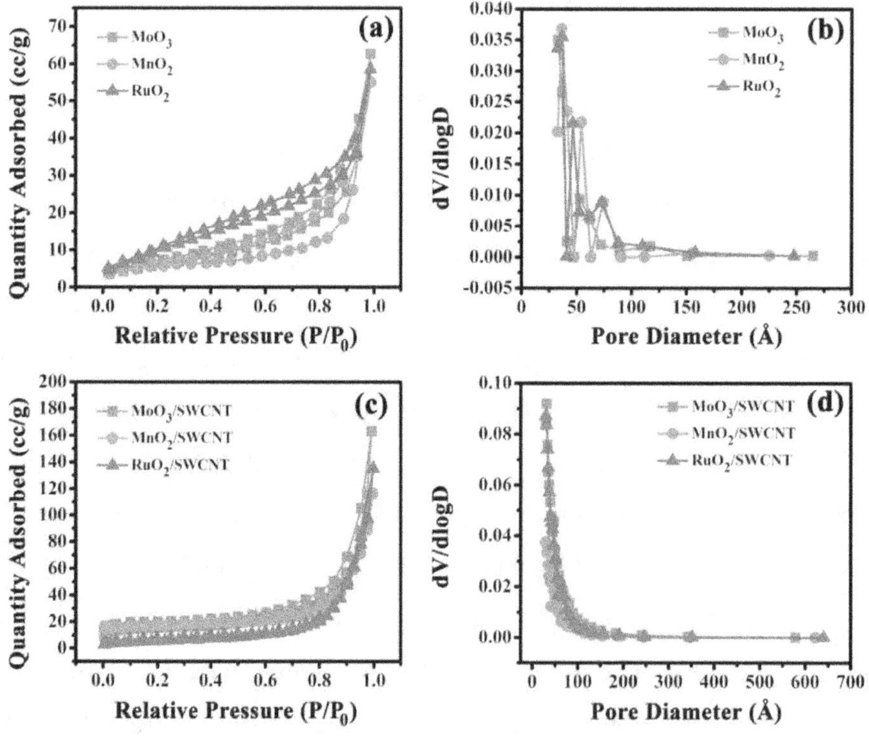

Fig. 4.15 (a,c) N_2 adsorption–desorption isotherms and (b,d) pore size distribution curves of the exfoliated MoO_3, MnO_2, RuO_2 nanosheets, and their composites with SWCNT respectively.

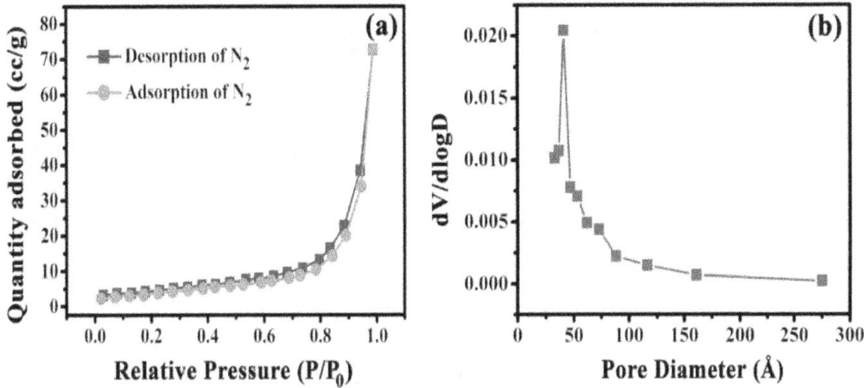

Figure4.16. Nitrogen adsorption-desorption isotherm (a)and corresponding pore size distribution curve (b) of the pristine SWCNTs.

4.5.3 Electrochemical study

4.5.3.1 Three electrodes measurement

We have systematically studied the electrochemical performance of the composite electrode materials both in two electrode and three electrode system. The as prepared thin films were transferred on gold coated PET for device fabrication. In the three electrode system we used Pt wire as a counter electrode, Ag/AgCl as a reference electrode and thin films on gold coated PET as a working electrode with 1 M Na_2SO_4 solution as a electrolyte. Cyclic voltammetry of the composite electrode materials were studied in the three electrode system (Figure 4.17) over the voltage window -1 to +1 V. The obtained specific capacitance values at 5 mv/s scan rate for the composite electrodes in three electrode systems are 1205.08F/g, 1168.69F/g and 1308.45F/g for MoO_3/SWCNT, MnO_2/SWCNT, and RuO_2/SWCNT electrodes respectively.

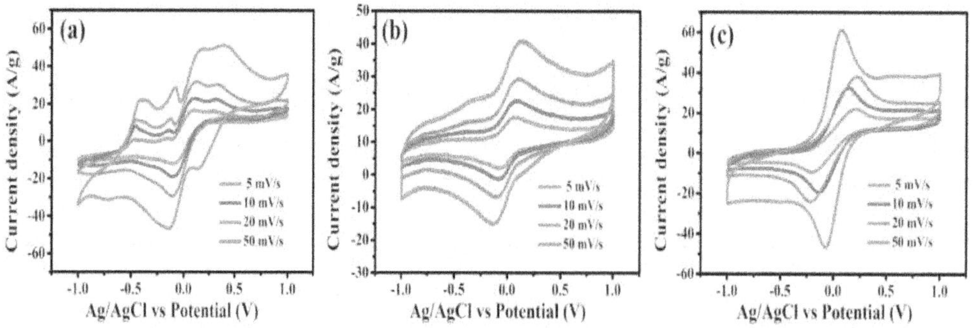

Figure.4.17 Cyclic voltammetry graph of (a) MoO$_3$/SWCNT,(b) MnO$_2$/SWCNT and (c) RuO$_2$/SWCNT at different scan rates respectively using three electrode system.

4.5.3.2 Two electrodes (Symmetric Solid State) Supercapacitor measurement

The symmetric solid state supercapacitors were prepared by these thin films with polyvinyl alcohol PVA-H$_2$SO$_4$ gel as a solid electrolyte sandwiched between the films. Cyclic voltammetry graph of the two electrode measurement for the composite electrode materials over the voltage window 0 V to +1 V shown in the Figure 4.18(a-c) at 5, 10, 20, 50, 100 mV/s scan rates. Galvanometric charging discharging performances of the two electrode system were also studied and are shown in the Figure 4.18(d-f). The maximum specific capacitance values at 5 mV/s scan rate are 717 F/g, 540 F/g, and 676 F/g for MoO$_3$/SWCNT, MnO$_2$/SWCNT and RuO$_2$/SWCNT electrodes respectively. Figure 4.18g shows that the specific capacitance decreases with scan rate for all three composites as expected.

The charge storage mechanism of the TMOs can be explained by following reversible redox reactions.

$$2MoO_3 + 2H^+ + 2e^- \leftrightarrow Mo_2O_5 \dots\dots\dots\dots\dots\dots\dots(3)$$

$$MnO_2 + H^+ + e^- \leftrightarrow MnOOH \dots\dots\dots\dots\dots\dots(4)$$

$$RuO_2 + \beta H^+ + \beta e \leftrightarrow RuO_{2-\beta}(OH)\beta \dots\dots\dots\dots(5)$$

The stability of the symmetric supercapacitors was also tested through a cyclic voltammetry at a fixed scan rate of 100mV/s for 1000 cycles. The symmetric supercapacitor device made by MoO$_3$/SWCNT electrodes retained 91.99 % of its initial specific capacitance value after 1000 CV cycles, whereas for the MnO$_2$/SWCNT and RuO$_2$/SWCNT symmetric supercapacitor are 95.88 % and 92.25 % respectively which indicative of excellent cycle stability of the symmetric supercapacitor devices as shown in the Figure 4.18h. The supercapacitor based on MoO$_3$/SWCNT composite electrode materials delivers a high energy density of 24.89Wh/Kg at a power density 1.61kW/kg. The RuO$_2$/SWCNT composite supercapacitor deliver energy density 23.48Wh/Kg at a power density 1.52kW/kg and that for MnO$_2$/SWCNT composite supercapacitor is 18.73Wh/Kg at a power density 1.21kW/kg. The Ragone plot of our devices and previously reported solid state supercapacitor devices is shown in the Figure 4.18(i). [73-78] We can see from the Ragone plot the performance of as prepared TMOs nanosheets/SWCNT composites are superior over previously reported metal oxide based supercapacitors in terms of specific capacitance and energy density.

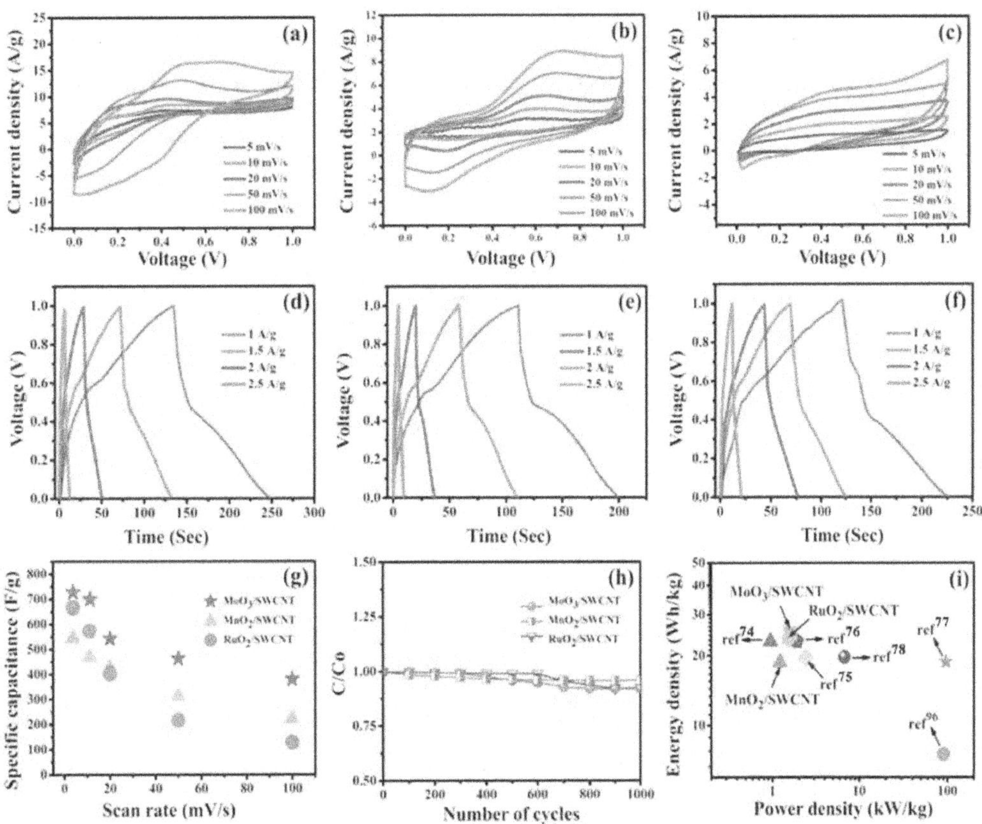

Figure. 4.18 Cyclic voltammetry graph of (a) MoO$_3$/SWCNT, (b) MnO$_2$/SWCNT and (c) RuO$_2$/SWCNT at different scan rates respectively; Galvanometric charging discharging graphs of (d) MoO$_3$/SWCNT, (e) MnO$_2$/SWCNT and (f) RuO$_2$/SWCNT at different current density respectively; (g) Scan rates vs specific capacitance graph of all TMOs/SWCNT composites; (h) C/C$_o$ vs number of cycles graph of all TMOs/SWCNT;

(i) Ragone plot for TMOs/SWCNT composites solid-state supercapacitor devices, compared with other reported metal oxides.

We have also studied the electrochemical impedance spectroscopy of all the solid state supercapacitors. The upper inset of (Figure 4.19) represents the schematic equivalent circuit model of the system, where R_s is the equivalent series resistance, R_{ct} is the charge transfer resistance, Zw is the Warburg impedance, Cl is the electric double capacitance. The obtained equivalent series resistances (R_s) from the Nyquist plot (Figure 4.19) are 1.85 Ω, 2.73 Ω and 2.43 Ω for MoO$_3$/SWCNT, MnO$_2$/SWCNT and RuO$_2$/SWCNT electrodes respectively. The absence of semicircles in the high frequency region even in the zoomed image (lower inset of Figure 4.19) indicates low charge transfer resistance of the electrodes implying rapid charge transfer at electrode-electrolyte interfaces. The size of the semi-circle of Nyquist plot is not only depends on the pseudo capacitive reactions; it's also governed by the oxide-substrate interface resistance.[79]

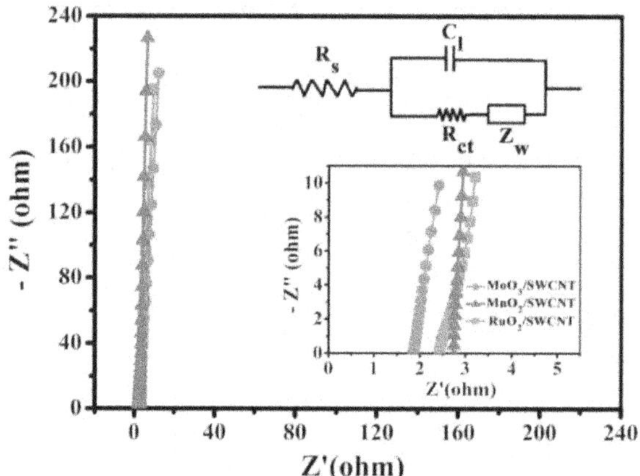

Figure 4.19. Nyquist plot of the all solid state supercapacitors; Inset showing the enlarge view of high frequency region and an equivalent circuit model.

Modern electronic devices are fast moving towards flexibility. To this end, we have investigated the behavior of our symmetric supercapacitors under a variety of bending conditions. The cyclic voltammetry of the solid state supercapacitors at different bending angle at 100 mV/s scan rate are shown in the Figure 4.20(a-c). The electrochemical performances of the device do not significantly change under various bending conditions. The specific capacitance values of the all the devices are almost remain same during bending, which is displayed in the Figure 4.20(d).

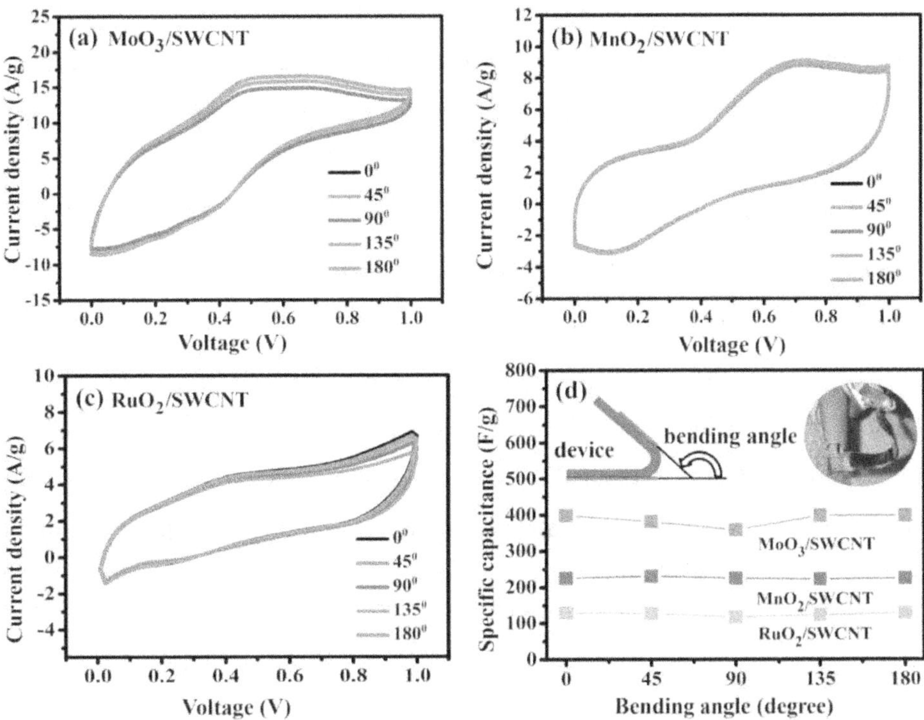

Figure.4.20 Cyclic voltammetry curves at different bending conditions at 100 mv/s scan rate for (a) MoO_3/SWCNT, (b) MnO_2/SWCNT and (c) RuO_2/SWCNT respectively.(d) Specific capacitance vs bending angle graph of all TMO/SWCNT composite.

4.5.3.1 Electrochemical study of In-plane Micro Supercapacitor based on MnO_2 and SWCNT

Fig.4.21 (a)-(f) shows the electrochemical performance of the as-fabricated in-plane supercapacitor based on MnO_2/SWCNT composite. Fig. 4.21(a) shows the cyclic voltrametry graph at different scan rates from 5mV/s to50 mV/s. The non-ideal rectangular shapes of the CV curves indicate the pseudo capacitive behaviors of the electrodes. The specific capacitances and areal capacitances of the in-plane supercapacitors were determined from the CV curves. The calculated areal capacitance values are 431.02 F/g, 365.85 F/g, 324.45 F/g,302.38 F/g, 290.15 F/g and 275 F/g at 5mv/s, 10 mV/s ,20 mV/s,30 mV/s,40 mV/s and 50 mV/s respectively. We have also calculated the corresponding areal capacitance values for different scan rates which are displays in the fig.4.21(c).Galvanometric charging discharging performances of the planar-supercapacitors also studied at different current density shown in the fig.4.21 (b). The obtained maximum specific capacitance is 560.22 F/g (5.25mF/cm^2) at 1.65A/g current density As fabricated planar-supercapacitor shows excellent stability displays in the fig.18(d), with 97.4% of the maximum capacitance retained after 1000 cycles. The calculated energy density is 77.80 Wh/kg (2.62 mWh/cm^2) at a power density 3.50kW/kg (43.66mW/cm^2). We also performed electrochemical impedance spectroscopy tests to evaluate the capacitive performances of the micro-capacitors. The larger slope of the straight line at low frequency region in Nyquist plot in fig.4.21(e) implies better capacitive behavior with a series resistance of ~33 ohm. The excellent mechanical flexibility of the planar supercapacitors is demonstrated in the fig.4.21(f).The CV curves at different bending angels at 0°, 45°, 90°, 135°, and 180° were almost overlapped, elucidate the superior flexibility and electrochemical stability.

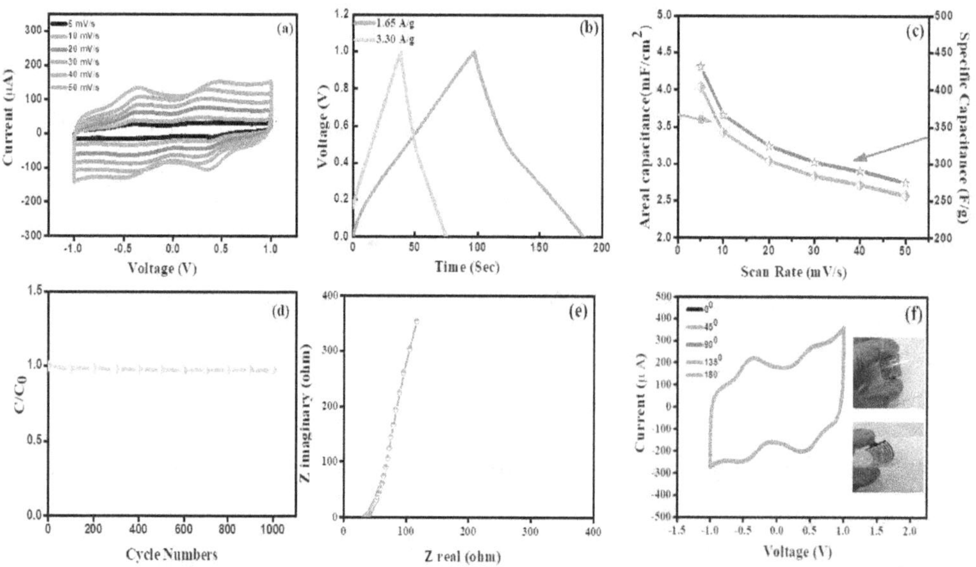

Figure 4.21. Cyclic voltammograms at different scan rates (a), Galvanostatic charge–discharge curves at different current density, (b) specific capacitance and areal cspacitance at different scan rates (c), Cycle stability graph (d), Nyquist plot(e), CV curves tested at 100 mV/s under different bending angels(f).

4.6 Summary

We have shown two poor solvents ethanol and water can be a good solvent for exfoliating TMOs when they combined in a particular volume fraction. This mixed solvent method is versatile, scalable and gives high concentration dispersion of TMOs nanosheets, higher than that reported previously. AFM and HRTEM study reveals that the nanosheets are mostly bi-layer with average lateral size of 300 nm for MoO_3 and 200 nm for MnO_2 and RuO_2 respectively. Raman and XPS study shows this method gives dispersion of defect free nanosheets of TMOs. Composite thin film of TMOs nanosheets with SWCNT (25 wt%) deposited of gold coated PET exhibited ultra-high capacitance (1205.08 F/g for MoO_3-SWNT) in three electrode system with aqueous Na_2SO_4 as electrolyte. As fabricated thin film symmetric supercapacitors in all-solid-state based on TMOs nanosheets composites with SWCNT with polyvinyl alcohol PVA–H_2SO_4 gel as a solid electrolyte exhibit high specific capacitance (717 F/g, 540 F/g and 676 F/g for MoO_3-SWCNT, MnO_2-SWCNT and RuO_2-SWCNT respectively), excellent flexibility and long cycle life, leading to an extremely high energy density (24.89 Wh/Kg at 1.61 kW/kg, 18.73 Wh/Kg at 1.21 kW/Kg and 23.48 Wh/Kg at 1.52 kW/Kg), whereas, in-plane micro supercapacitors based on few layered MnO_2 and SWCNT hybrid displayed excellent specific capacitance of 560.22 F/g with significant energy density of 77.80 Wh/kg and excellent cycling stability even after 1000 cycles. Our findings represent a promising direction and significant steps towards exfoliating TMOs to produce 2D oxide nanosheets in low toxic mixed solvent for flexible energy storage device with high energy density.

4.7. References

1. W. Tang, L. Liu, S. Tian, L. Li, Y. Yue, Y. Wu and K. Zhu, *Chem. Commun.,* 2011, **47**,10058-10060.

2. F. Luan, G. Wang, Y. Ling, X. Lu, H. Wang, Y. Tong, X.X. Liu and Y. Li, *Nanoscale,* 2013, **5**, 7984-7990.

3. L.K. Naslund, A. S. Ingason, S. Holmin and J. Rosen, *J. Phys. Chem. C,* 2014, **28**, 15315-15323.

4. X. Lu, G. Wang, T. Zhai, M. Yu, J. Gan, Y. Tong and Y. Li, *Nano Lett.,* 2012, **12**, 1690-1696.

5. X. Lu, T. Zhai, X. Zhang, Y. Shen, L. Yuan, B. Hu, L. Gong, J. Chen, Y. Gao, J. Zhou, Y.Tong and Z. L. Wang, *Adv. Mater.,* 2012, **24**, 938-944.

6. G. Yu, L. Hu, N. Liu, H. Wang, M. Vosgueritchian, Y. Yang, Y. Cui and Z. Bao, *Nano Lett.,* 2011, **11**, 4438-4442.

7. Y. Zhao, Y. Meng, H. Wu, Y. Wang, Z. Wei, X. Li and P. Jiang, *RSC Adv.,* 2015, **5**, 90307-90312.

8. L. Wu, R. Li, J. Guo, C. Zhou, W. Zhang, C. Wang, Y. Huang, Y. Li and J. Liu, *AIP Adv.*, 2013, **3**, 082129.

9. L. Peng, X. Peng, B. Liu, C. Wu, Y. Xie and G. Yu, *Nano Lett.*, 2013, **13**, 2151-2157.

10. J. Feng, X. Sun, C. Wu, L. Peng, C. Lin, S. Hu, J. Yang and Y. Xie, *J. Am. Chem. Soc.*, 2011, **133**, 17832-17838.

11. J. Xie, X. Sun, N. Zhang, K. Xu, M. Zhou and Y. Xie, *Nano Energy*, 2013, **2**, 65-74.

12. J. Yan, Z. Fan, W. Sun, G. Ning, T. Wei, Q. Zhang, R. Zhang, L. Zhi and F. Wei, *Adv. Funct.Mater.*, 2012, **22**, 2632-2641.

13. V. Gupta, T. Kusahara, H. Toyama, S. Gupta and N. Miura, *Electrochem. Commun.*, 2007, **9**, 2315-2319.

14. H. Wang, Q. Hao, X. Yang, L. Lu and X. Wang, *Nanoscale*, 2010, **2**, 2164-2170.

15. K. Jurewicz, S. Delpeux, V. Bertagna, F. Beguin and E. Frackowiak, *Chem. Phys. Lett.*, 2001, **347**, 36-40.

16. J. Tao, N. Liu, W. Ma, L. Ding, L. Li, J. Su and Y. Gao, *Sci. Rep.*, 2013, **3**, 2286.

17. A. Laforgue, P. Simon, C. Sarrazin and J.F. Fauvarque, *J. Power Sources.* 1999, **80**, 142-148.

18. L. Pan, G. Yu, D. Zhai, H. R. Lee, W. Zhao, N. Liu, H. Wang, B. C. K. Tee, Y. Shi, Y. Cui and Z. Bao, *Proc. Natl. Acad. Sci. U. S. A.*, 2012, **109**, 9287-9292.

19. J. J. Yoo, K. Balakrishnan, J. Huang, V. Meunier, B. G. Sumpter, A. Srivastava, M. Conway, A. L. M. Reddy, J. Yu, R. Vajtai and P. M. Ajayan, *Nano Lett.*, 2011, **11**, 1423-1427.

20. X. Huang, X. Qi, F. Boey and H. Zhang, *Chem. Soc. Rev.*, 2012, **41**, 666-686.

21. A. K. Geim and K. S. Novoselov, *Nat. Mater.*, 2007, **6**, 183-191.

22. X. Huang, C.Tan, Z. Yin and H. Zhang, *Adv. Mater.*, 2014, **26**, 2185-2204.

23. F. Bonaccorso, L. Colombo, G. Yu, M. Stoller, V. Tozzini, A. C. Ferrari, R. S. Ruoff and V. Pellegrini, *Science,* 2015, **41**, 347.

24. S. Dutta, S. Pal and S. De, *New J. Chem.*, 2018, **42**, 10161-10166.

25. G. Wang, X.G. Zhu, Y.Y. Sun, Y.Y. Li, T. Zhang, J. Wen, X.Chen, K. He, L.L. Wang, X.C. Ma, J.F. Jia, S. B. Zhang and Q.K. Xue, *Adv. Mater.*, 2011, **23**, 2929-2932.

26. C. Y. Zhi, Y. Bando, C. C. Tang, H. Kuwahara and D. Golberg, *Adv. Mater.*, 2009, **21**, 2889-2893.

27. B. Radisavljevic, A. Radenovic, J. Brivio, V. Giacometti and A. Kis, *Nat. Nanotechnol.,* 2011, **6**, 147-150.

28. W. J. Yu, S. Y. Lee, S. H. Chae, D. Perello, G. H. Han, M. Yun and Y. H. Lee, *Nano Lett.,* 2011, **11**, 1344-1350.

29. S. Yin, Y. Zhang, J. Kong, C. Zou, C. M. Li, X. Lu, J. Ma, F. Y. C. Boey and X. Chen, *ACS Nano,* 2011, **5**, 3831-3838.

30. K. Chang and W. Chen, *ACS Nano*, 2011, **5**, 4720-4728.

31. J. Jiang, Y. Li , J. Liu , X. Huang , C. Yuan and X. W. Lou, *Adv. Mater.,* 2012, **24**, 5166-5180.

32. C. C. Hu, W. C. Chen and K. H. Chang, *J. Electrochem. Soc.,* 2004, **151**, A281-A290.

33. Y. T. Kim, K. Tadai and T. Mitani , *J. Mater. Chem.,* 2005, **1**, 4914-4921.

34. L. Peng, P. Xiong, L. Ma, Y. Yuan, Y. Zhu, D. Chen, X. Luo, J. Lu, K. Amine and G. Yu, *Nat.Commun.,* 2017, **8**, 15139.

35. R.J. Smith, P.J. King, M. Lotya, C. Wirtz, U. Khan, S. De, A. O'Neill, G.S. Duesberg, J.C. Grunlan, G. Moriarty, J. Chen, J. Wang, A. Minett, V. Nicolosi and J.N. Coleman, *Adv. Mater.,*2011, **23**, 3944-3948.

36. J.N. Coleman, M. Lotya, A.O' Neill, S.D. Bergin, P.J. King, U. Khan, K. Young, A. Gaucher and S. De, *Science,* 2011, **331**, 568-571.

37. M. Lotya, P.J. King, U. Khan, S. De and J.N. Coleman, *ACS Nano,* 2010, **4**, 3155-3162.

38. U. Khan, A.O' Neill, M. Lotya, S. De and J. N Coleman, *Small,* 2010, **6**, 864-871.

39. M. Lotya, Y. Hernandez, P.J. King, R.J. Smith, V. Nicolosi, L.S. Karlsson, F.M. Blighe and S.De, *J. Am. Chem. Soc.,* 2009, **131**, 3611-3620.

40. Y. Hernandez, V. Nicolosi, M. Lotya, F. M. Blighe, Z. Sun, S. De, I. T. McGovern, B. Holland, M. Byrne, Y. K. Gun'Ko, J. J. Boland, P. Niraj, G. Duesberg, S. Krishnamurthy, R. Goodhue, J. Hutchison, V. Scardaci, A. C. Ferrari and J. N. Coleman, *Nat. Nanotech.,* 2008, **3**, 563–568.

41. D. Hanlon, C. Backes, T. M. Higgins, M. Hughes, A. O'Neill, P. King, N. McEvoy, G. S. Duesberg, B. M. Sanchez, H. Pettersson, V. Nicolosi and J. N. Coleman, *Chem. Mater.,* 2014, **26**, 1751–1763.

42. P. Blake, P. D. Brimicombe, R. R. Nair, T. J. Booth, D. Jiang, F. Schedin, L. A. Ponomarenko, S. V. Morozov, H. F. Gleeson, E. W. Hill, A. K. Geim and K. S. Novoselov, *Nano Lett.,* 2008, **8**, 1704-1708.

43. X. Cui, C. Z.Zhang, R. Hao and Y. L. Hou, *Nanoscale,* 2011, **3**, 2118-2126.

44. G. Cunningham, M.Lotya, C.S. Cucinotta, S.Sanvito and S. D. Bergin, *ACS Nano,* 2012, **6**, 3468-3480.

45. K.G. Zhou, N.N. Mao, H.X. Wang, Y. Peng and H.L. Zhang, *Angew. Chem. Int. Ed.,* 2011, **50**, 10839-10842.

46. A. A. Green and M. C. Hersam, *Nano Lett.,* 2009, **9**, 4031-4036.

47. A. B. Bourlinos, V. Georgakilas and R. Zboril, *Solid State Commun.,* 2009, **149**, 2172-2176.

48. P. May, U. Khan, J.M. Hughes and J. N. Coleman, *J. Phys. Chem. C.,* 2012, **116**, 11393-11400.

49. A. O'Neill, U. Khan, P. N. Nirmalraj, J. Boland and J. N. Coleman, *J. Phys. Chem. C,* 2011, **115**, 5422-5428.

50. C. M. Hansen, *CRC, Boca Raton,* 2007.

51. J. N. Coleman, *Adv. Funct. Mater.* 2009, **19**, 3680-3695.

52. K. Kai, Y. Yoshida, H. Kageyama, G. Saito, T. Ishigaki, Y. Furukawa and J. Kawamata, *J. Am. Chem. Soc.,* 2008, **130**, 15938-15943.

53. K. Kalantar-zadeh, J. Tang, M. Wang, K. L. Wang, A. Shailos, K. Galatsis, R.Kojima, V. Strong, A. Lech, W. Wlodarski and R. B. Kaner, *Nanoscale,* 2010, **2**, 429-433.

54. M. Osada and T. Sasaki, *J. Mater. Chem.,* 2009, **19**, 2503-2511.

55. S.J. Choi, J.S. Jang, H. J.Park and I.D. Kim, *Adv. Funct. Mater.,* 2017, 1606026.

56. Y. Wang, Y. Zhu, Z.Xing and Y.Qian, *Int. J. Electrochem. Sci.,* 2013, **8**, 9851-9857.

57. Y. Chen, C. Lu, L. Xu, Y. Ma, W. Hou and J.J. Zhu, *CrystEngComm.,* 2010, **12**, 3740-3747.

58. X. Zhang, P. Yu, H. Zhang, D. Zhang, X. Sun and Y. Ma, *Electrochim. Acta,* 2013, **89**, 523-529.

59. J. Zhou, L. Yu, M. Sun, S. Yang, F. Ye, J. He and Z. Hao, *Ind. Eng. Chem. Res.,* 2013, **52**, 9586-9593.

60. J. Liu, J. Jiang, C. Cheng, H. Li, J. Zhang, H. Gong and H. J. Fan, *Adv. Mater.,* 2011, **23**, 2076-2081.

61. N. Soin, S.S. Roy, C.O Kane, T.H. Lim, C.J.D. Hetherington and J.A. McLaughlin, *CrystEngComm.*, 2011, **13**, 312-318.

62. N. Soin, S. S. Roy, T. H. Lim and J. A. D. McLaughlin, *J. Mater. Chem.*, 2011, **129**, 1051-1057.

63. J.X. Wang, S.R. Brankovic, Y. Zhu, J.C. Hanson and R.R. Adzi, *J. Electrochem. Soc.*, 2003, **150**, A1108-A1117.

64. T. Siciliano, A. Tepore, E. Filippo, G. Micocci and M. Tepore, *Mater. Chem. Phys.*, 2009, **114**, 687.

65. A. Ogata, S. Komaba, R. Baddour-Hadjean, J.P. Pereira-Ramos and N. Kumagai, *Electrochim Acta*, 2008, **53**, 3084-3093.

66. S. Y. Mar, C. S. Chen, Y. S. Huang and K. K. Tiong, *Appl. Surf. Sci.*, 1995, **90**, 497-504.

67. B. Mendoza-Sánchez and P. S. Grant,. *Electrochim. Acta*, 2013, **98**, 294-302.

68. Y.C. Lin, W. Zhang, J.K. Huang, K.K. Liu, Y.H. Lee, C.T. Liang, C.W. Chu and L.J. Li, *Nanoscale*, 2012, **4**, 6637-6641.

69. R. S. Kalubarme, Y.H. Kim and C.J. Park, *Nanotechnology*, 2013, **24**, 365401.

70. B. Wu, C. Wang, Y. Cui, L. Mao and S. Xiong, *RSC Adv.*, 2015, **5**, 16986-16992.

71. J.C. Chou, Y.L. Chen, M.H. Yang, Y.Z. Chen, C.C. Lai, H.T. Chiu, C.Y. Lee, Y.L. Chueh and J.Y. Gan, *J. Mater. Chem. A*, 2013, **1**, 8753-8758.

72. H. Xia, M. Lai and L. Lu, *J. Mater. Chem.*, 2010, **20**, 6896-6902.

73. Y. Shao, H. Wang, Q. Zhang and Y. Li, *J. Mater. Chem. C*, 2013, **1**, 1245-1251.

74. J. Yang, G. Li, Z. Pan, M. Liu, Y. Hou, Y. Xu, H. Deng, L. Sheng, X. Zhao, Y. Qiu and Y.Zhang, *ACS Appl. Mater. Interfaces*, 2015, **7**, 22172-22180.

75. H. Su, P. Zhu, L. Zhang, F. Zhou, G. Li, T. Li, Q. Wang, R. Sun and C. Wong, *J. Electroanal. Chem.*, 2017, **786**, 28-34.

76. P.C. Chen, H.T. Chen, J. Qiu and C.W. Zhou, *Nano Res.*, 2010, **3**, 594-603.

77. B.G. Choi, S.J Chang, H.W. Kang, C.P. Park, H.J. Kim, W.H. Hong, S. Lee and Y.S. Huh, *Nanoscale*, 2012, **4**, 4983-4988.

78. J. Duay, E. Gillette, R. Liu and S.B. Lee, *Phys. Chem.*, 2012, **14**, 3329-3337.

79. A. Allison and H.A. Andreas, *J. Power Sources.*, 2019, **426**, 93–96.

Chapter5

BiVO$_4$–Reduce Graphene Oxide Nanocomposite based Supercapacitor with Excellent Cycle Stability

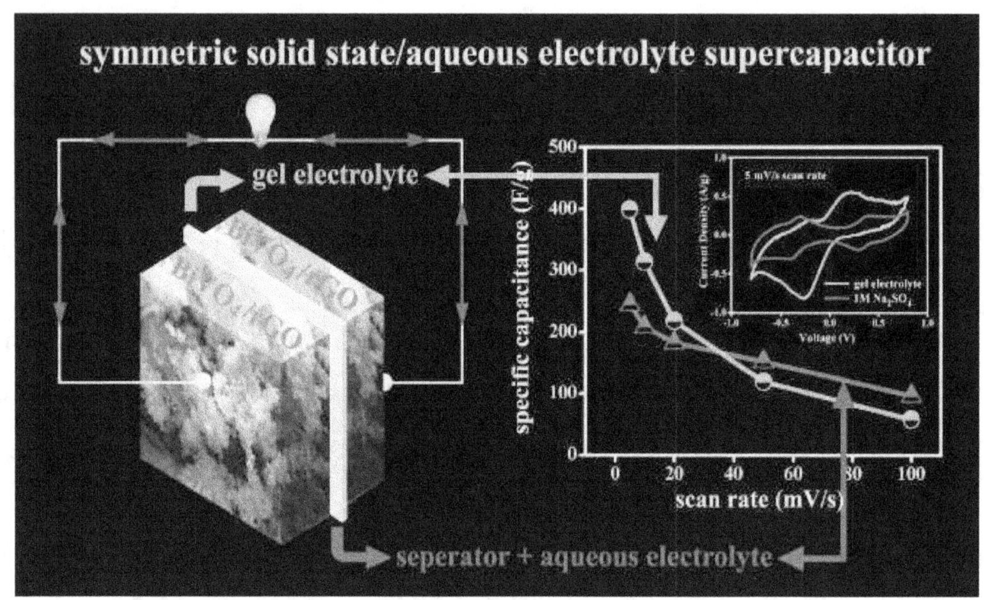

Work presented in this chapter has been published in:

New J. Chem., 2018, 42, 10161-10166

Shibsankar Dutta, Shreyasi Pal, Sukanta De

5.1. Introduction

In this chapter we demonstrate the synthesis of $BiVO_4$/rGO hybrid nanostructure by a simple hydrothermal method. Symmetric cell based on this hybrid nanostructure was fabricated and tested electrochemical properties in both PVA/H_2SO_4 gel and aqueous Na_2SO_4 electrolyte. $BiVO_4$/rGO hybrid based symmetric supercapacitor exhibits better performance in solid electrolyte with high specific capacitance of 400 F/g at 5mV/s and excellent energy density of 35.37 Wh/kg. The as fabricated symmetric supercapacitor shows excellent stability which retains 98% of its initial capacitance after 1000 cycles.

In the last few decades, Compare to the individual transition metal oxides, binary transition metal oxides such as $MnWO_4$,[7] $NiCo_2O_4$,[8] $CoMoO_4$-$NiMoO_4$,[9] $NiMoO_4$,[10] $MnCo_2O_4$,[11] ZnV_2O_4,[12] $LiZnVO_4$,[13] $ZnFe_2O_4$,[14] $CuCo_2O_4$,[15] and $ZnCo_2O_4$[16] grasped enormous attention to the researchers for their excellent electrochemical performance due to their high conductivity and higher electrochemical activity.

It has been already seen that bismuth-based nanostructured materials have caught researcher's great attention due to their applications in semiconductors, catalysts and biomedicine. Among these bismuth family materials, narrow band gaped; bismuth vanadate ($BiVO_4$) has received great attention due to their wide range of applications in ferroelectrics, photocatalytic activity, photochemical solar cells etc.[7-10] To date, crystalline bismuth vanadates has been prepared by a variety of synthesis methods, including solid state reaction, hydrothermal treatment, sonochemistry and metalorganic decomposition and co-precipitation process.[10-13]. Preparation of well crystalline monoclinic $BiVO_4$ can be possible by simple hydrothermal route due to which hydrothermal process is the first choice to the researcher among the different synthesis process. $BiVO_4$ is an electro-active metal oxide which is novel candidate for energy storage applications due to its unique properties. However, $BiVO_4$ suffer from lower electrical conductivity which can be improved by forming a hybrid or composite with conducting materials and for this purpose different porous and conducting carbon materials are the good choice. Khan and his co-worker already reported that 20 Wt% SWCNT based BiVO4 composite electrodes exhibited the specific capacitance value 395 F/g at 2.5 A/g.[14] Patil et al. reported fern like $BiVO_4$/rGO composite obtained specific capacitance 151 F/g under the current density of 0.15 mA/cm^2.[15] Arora and her co-worker reported MoS_2/$BiVO_4$ composites supercapacitor delivered specific capacitance 610 F/g at 1A/g current density.[16]

5.2. Experimental

The $BiVO_4$ nanoparticles were prepared by simple hydrothermal route.[18] In the details synthesis 4.90 g $Bi(NO_3)_3.5H_2O$ was added to the 20 ml 4mol.dm^{-3} HNO_3 solution, whereas 1.85g Na_3VO_4 was added to the 20 ml 2mol.dm^{-3} NaOH solution. Then 0.25 g SDS was added to each the above solutions. After 30 min stirring mixed the as prepared solutions. The pH value of the mixture was then adjusted to 7 adding 2mol.dm^{-3} NaOH solution under vigorous stirring and kept it for another 30 min. Finally precursor solution was transferred into a Teflon-lined stainless steel autoclave and kept it at 200 °C for 90 min. After the autoclave was cooled to room temperature and the precipitate was washed by D.I. water and ethanol several times and kept at 100 °C for 4 h. The time variation of the above experiment was also performed keeping all other parameters same. Henceforth, we designate the samples corresponding to 30 min, 60 min, 90 min and 120 min reaction span as B-30, B-60, B-90 and B-120 respectively. In the present reaction due to the hydrolysis of $Bi(NO_3)_3.5H_2O$, soluble $BiONO_3$ was initially formed which reacted with the VO^{3-} ions provided by Na_3VO_4 at pH ~7 and formed the yellow precipitate of tetragonal $BiVO_4$. In the above reaction pH of the solution was controlled by the NaOH. For the duration of hydrothermal treatment, the formed $BiVO_4$ nuclei were converted to the well crystalline structure of monoclinic $BiVO_4$ nanocrystals. The probable reactions taking place in the BiVO4 formation are shown below

$$Bi(NO_3)_3.5H_2O + HNO_3 + H_2O \rightarrow BiONO_3 + 3HNO_3 \qquad (1)$$

$$BiONO_3 + Na_3VO_4 + H_2O \rightarrow BiVO_4 + NaNO_3 + NaOH \qquad (2)$$

For the synthesis of $BiVO_4$/rGO hybrids, graphene oxide (GO) was prepared by modified Hummers method.[17] to prepare different $BiVO_4$/rGO hybrids, different concentration of GO solution (20 mL, 40 mL and 60 mL) with initial concentration (1mg/mL) was added to the above mentioned mixture and kept at hydrothermal reaction at 200 °C for 90 min. Henceforth we denote the $BiVO_4$/rGO samples using 20 mg, 40 mg and 60 mg of GO contents as the BG1, BG2 and BG3.

5.3 Characterizations

Powder X-ray diffraction (XRD) patterns of the as prepared samples were recorded to determine the phase formation and purity using Rigaku-Ultima III X-ray diffractometer with CuKα radiation (λ = 1.5418 Å). Raman spectra were obtained using spectrometer IHR550 and the laser of excitation wavelength 532 nm, The Surface morphology and microstructure of the as prepared materials were characterized by FESEM (HITACHI

S-4800), TEM (JEOL- 2010) and X-ray photoelectron spectroscopy (XPS) of the prepared materials were obtained by SPECS HSA-3500 hemispherical analyzer with monochromatic Mg Kα X-ray source.

5.4. Results and discussion

5.4.1. Structural & morphological analysis:

The micrograph of the sample for a nominal growth time of 30 min (B-30) shows that few undeveloped structures consists with particulate nature start to form (Fig.5.1a). However, for the increase of reaction time no specific shape was formed within 60 min duration (B-60) which is cleared from Fig. 5.1b. For the optimum growth duration of 90 min (sample B-90), well distributed $BiVO_4$ nanoparticles having almost same in shape and size with an average dimension of ~20–30 nm are formed (Fig.5.1c). Further prolonging the reaction span up to 120 min for sample B-120, $BiVO_4$ nanoparticles are agglomerated and attached together to form larger particles of irregular dimensions (Fig.5.1d). Fig.5.2 shows the FESEM images of $BiVO_4$/rGO hybrids revealing the presence of both the $BiVO_4$ nanoparticles and rGO thin sheets. Fig.5.2 shows the FESEM images of $BiVO_4$/rGO hybrids, where the thin sheets of rGO are well wrapped with the $BiVO_4$ (B-90) nanoparticles.

Figure 5.1: FESEM images of (a) B-30, (b) B-60, (c) B-90 and (d) B-120 samples; insets showing their high magnification view.

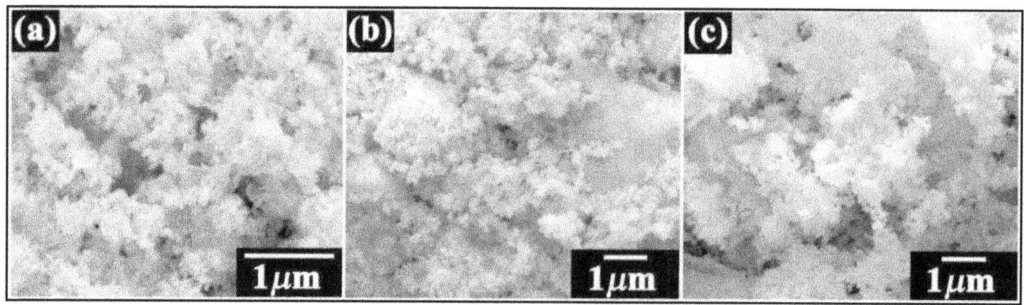

Figure 5.2: FESEM images of (a) BG1, (b) BG2, (c) BG3 samples.

The XRD patterns of all $BiVO_4$ samples that were synthesized under various conditions presented in Fig.5.3(a) also confirm the phase purity of samples. The XRD pattern of the as synthesized $BiVO_4$ indicates the formation of pure phase monoclinic crystal structure of $BiVO_4$ and the peaks could be indexed according to the previously reported data (JCPDS# 014-0688).

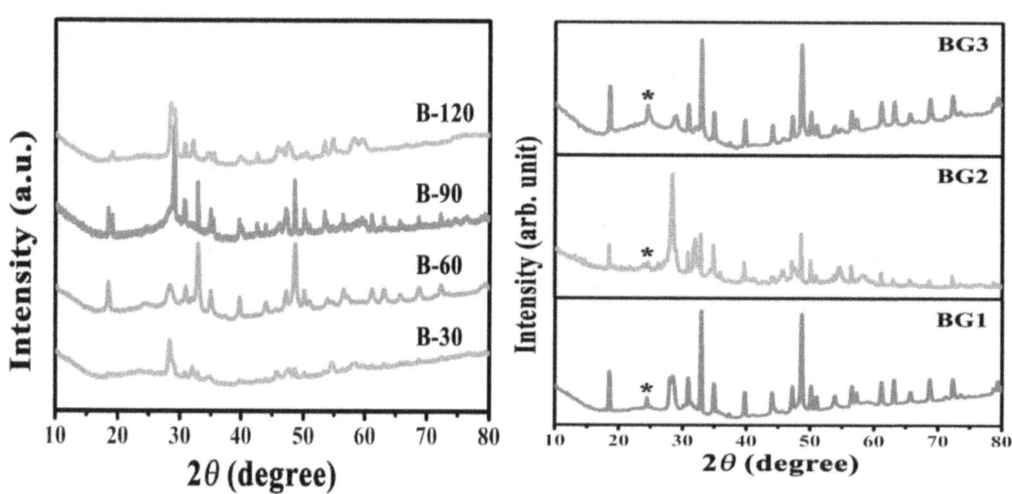

Figure 5.3: XRD pattern of $BiVO_4$ samples synthesized at different reaction time(a), $BiVO_4$/rGO samples with GO concentration variation(b).

In case of $BiVO_4$/rGO hybrids the diffraction peaks (*) correspond to rGO was observed at 2θ~ 25.1° confirms the presence of rGO in the samples (Fig. 5.3 b). Further, FESEM and XRD results reveals that among the all samples B90 and BG2 was well crystalline than others. Fig.5.4represented XRD patterns of well crystalline B90 and BG2.

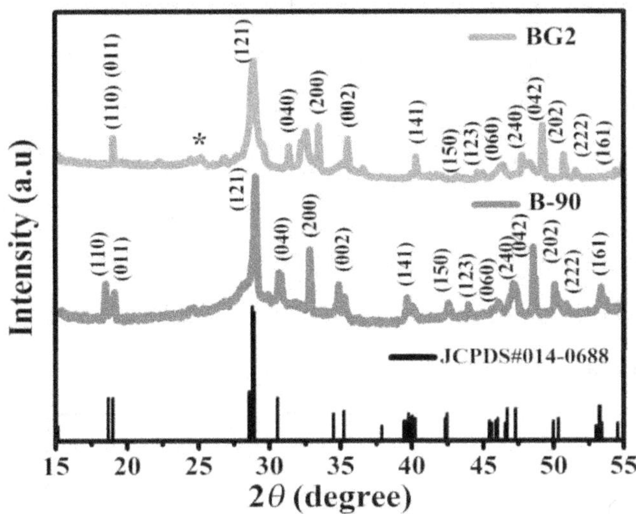

Figure 5.4: XRD patterns of BiVO$_4$ nanoparticles (B-90) and BiVO$_4$/rGO hybrids (BG2)

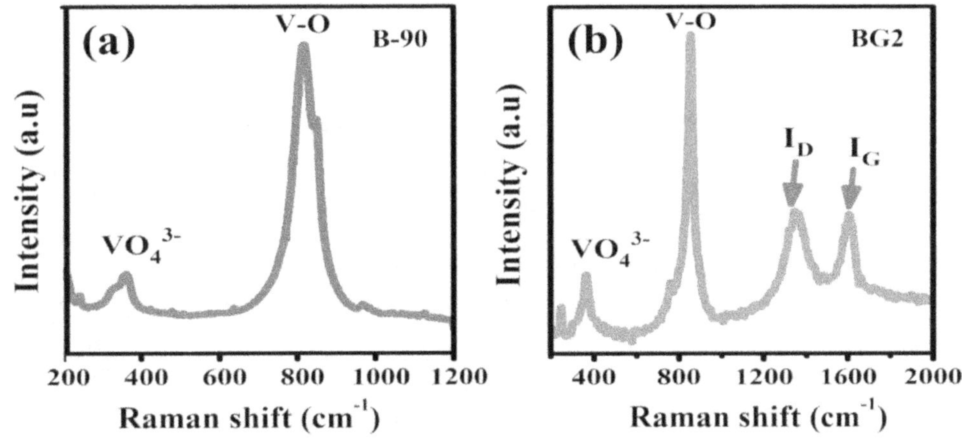

Figure 5.5: Raman spectra of B-90 and BG2.

Fig.5.5 depicts the Raman spectra of the as prepared B-90 and BG2 samples. The most intense peak at 830 cm^{-1} corresponds to the stretching modes of V-O band and the asymmetric and symmetric deformation modes of VO$_4^{3-}$ are also present at 330 and 373 cm^{-1} respectively.[19] The bands at 1351 and 1581 cm^{-1} are assigned to D and G band of rGO also present in BiVO$_4$/rGO hybrid. The obtained D to G peak intensity ratio (I_D/I_G) is 1.16 indicating the formation of rGO in hybrid materials which also substantiates the XRD result.

X-ray photoelectron spectroscopy (XPS) has been analyzed to explicate the surface composition and chemical state of the B-90 sample. The XPS survey scan of

BiVO$_4$ indicates that the sample is consisted with Bi, V, C, and O only (Fig.5.6). The high resolution spectrum of C 1s at 284.6 eV corresponds to the adventitious carbon (Fig.5.8a) [20]. The XPS spectra of O 1s (Fig.5.8b) having two peaks at 528.5 and 531.4 eV is attributed to the lattice oxygen of BiVO$_4$ and the adsorbed H$_2$O or surface hydroxyl groups respectively. [21] The spin-orbit splitting of Bi 4f peaks exhibits two symmetrical peaks located at 158.2 and 163.5 eV assigning to be Bi 4f$_{7/2}$ and Bi 4f$_{5/2}$ respectively, confirms the Bi^{3+} state of BiVO$_4$ sample (Fig.5.8c). [21] The high resolution spectrum of V 2p (Fig.5.8d) presents two peaks at 524.8 eV (V 2p$_{1/2}$) and 516.8 eV (V 2p$_{3/2}$), indicating that V species exists as V^{5+} in are in BiVO$_4$. [21]

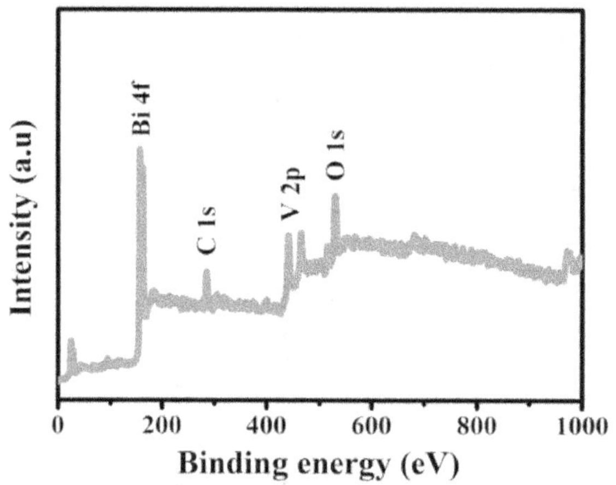

Figure 5.6: XPS survey scan of B-90 sample.

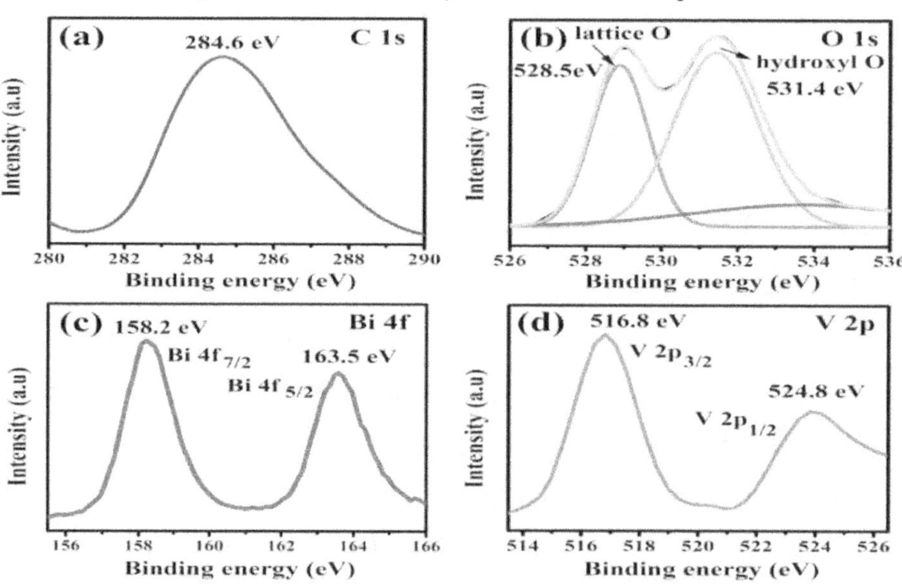

Figure 5.7: High resolution XPS spectra of (a) C 1s, (b) O 1s, (c) Bi 4f and (d) V 2P for the B-90 sample.

Fig.5.8a depicts the low magnification transmission electron microscopy (TEM) images of prepared B-90 sample. The high resolution TEM image of the sample displays the clear lattice fringe which indicates the high crystallinity of $BiVO_4$. The high resolution TEM (HRTEM) provides lattice spacing of 0.255 nm, which corresponds to the (020) lattice plane of monoclinic $BiVO_4$ (Fig.5.8b).[9] Further selected area electron diffraction (SAED) pattern consisting with bright circular spots suggests the single crystalline nature (Fig. 5.8b inset) of $BiVO_4$ sample.[22]

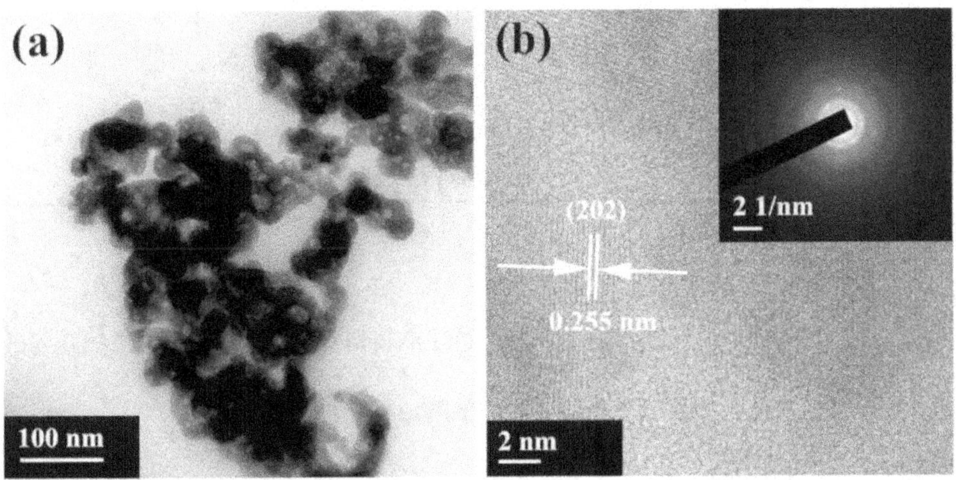

Figure 5.8: (a) Low magnification TEM and (b) HRTEM images of B-90 sample. Inset shows the SAED patterns.

5.4.2: Electrochemical study:

We have studied the cyclic voltammetry (CV) performances of the B-30, B-60, B-90 and B-120 samples at 5 mV/s scan rate in two electrode configuration using both 1M Na_2SO_4 aqueous electrolyte and PVA/H_2SO_4 gel as solid electrolyte (Fig.5.9).

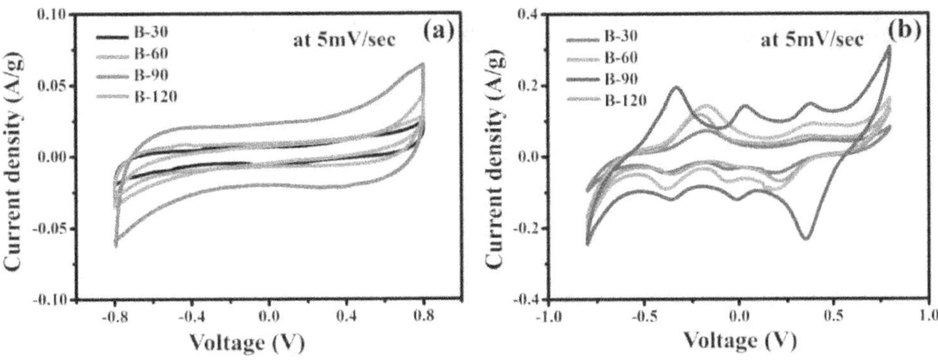

Figure 5.9: CV graphs of all $BiVO_4$ samples using both (a) 1 M Na_2SO_4 aqueous electrolyte and (b) PVA/H_2SO_4 gel electrolyte respectively.

Amongst the all samples, B-90 exhibits superior electrochemical performance due to their high surface area and well crystalline nature which is obvious from our FESEM and XRD results. Then the CV performances of all the hybrid samples BG1, BG2 and BG3 are also carried out in both the electrolytes in two electrode configurations (Fig.5.10).

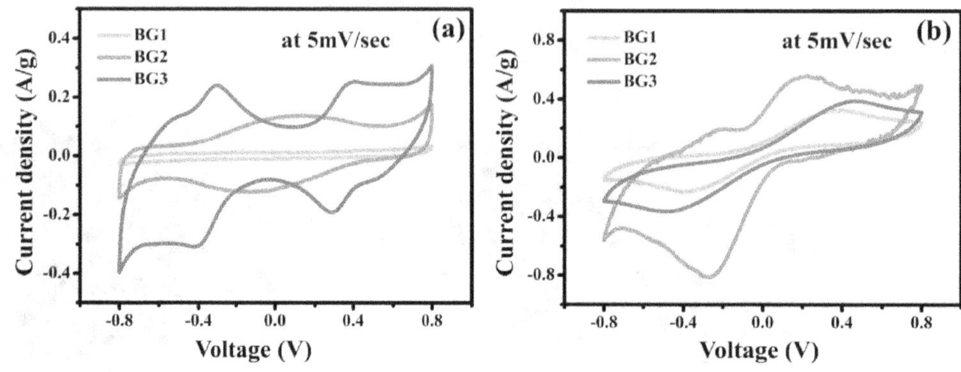

Figure 5.10: CV graphs of the BiVO$_4$/rGO hybrids using both (a) 1 M Na$_2$SO$_4$ aqueous electrolyte and (b) PVA/H$_2$SO$_4$ gel electrolyte respectively.

The enhanced electrochemical performance of BiVO$_4$/rGO hybrid electrodes over B-90 electrode can be attributed to the synergistic effect of hybrid nanostructure as in hybrids presence of rGO sheets make it more porous which ultimately promote electrolyte access and exposure of active sites to the electrolyte. Also the conducting nature of rGO widely controls the capacitive behavior of BiVO$_4$ in the hybrid electrodes providing easy access of electron transport reducing internal resistances. The specific capacitance values for all the as synthesized BiVO$_4$ and BiVO$_4$/rGO samples in two electrode configurations is displayed in Fig.5.11 and based on cyclic voltammetry performance supremacy we choose B-90 and BG2 samples for further electrochemical studies.

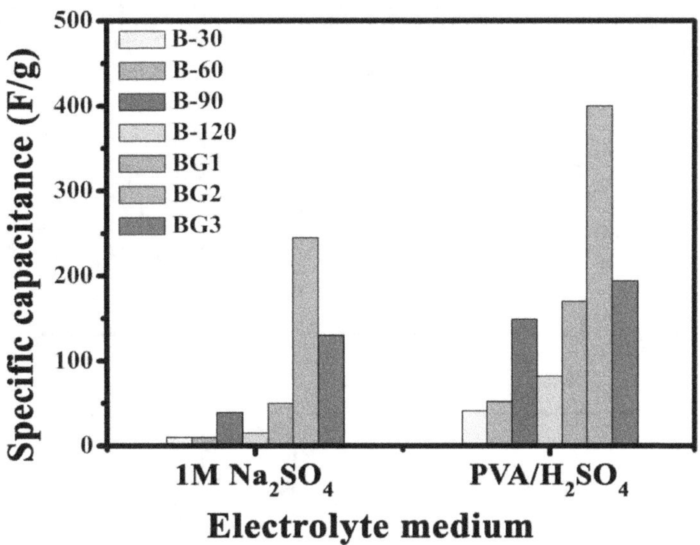

Figure 5.11: Electrochemical performance of all the BiVO₄ and BiVO₄/rGO hybrids electrodes under investigation.

Fig.5.12a represents the CV curves of the hybrid electrode (BG2) at different scan rates in solid (PVA/H_2SO_4 gel) electrolyte with a wider voltage window from -0.8 V to +0.8 V. CV curves of both B-90 and BG2 hybrid at 5 mV/s scan rate are shown in the Fig.5.12b. Well defined redox peaks are observed for CV curves of both B-90 and hybrids (BG2) at different scan rates indicating the strong pseudo-capacitive nature of electrode materials. The reversible faradic reactions occurred in the electrodes corresponding to the redox pairs V(4)/V(5) [15]. The probable reaction mechanism may be express as follows: [23]

$$BiVO_p + q\,M^+ + qe^- \leftrightarrow V_{2p-q}\,O_p M_q^{q+} \qquad \text{(Where } M^+ = \text{Electrolyte ions)} \qquad (1)$$

The specific capacitance of hybrid electrode using PVA/H_2SO_4 solid electrolyte at different scan rate is shown in Fig.5.13c. The obtained maximum specific capacitance value is 400 F/g at 5 mV/s scan rate for the hybrid electrode materials and that for B-90 electrode materials is 149 F/g at same scan rate. The calculated specific capacitance values of the hybrid electrode are 314, 218, 119 and 58 F/g at 10, 20, 50 and 100 mV/s respectively.

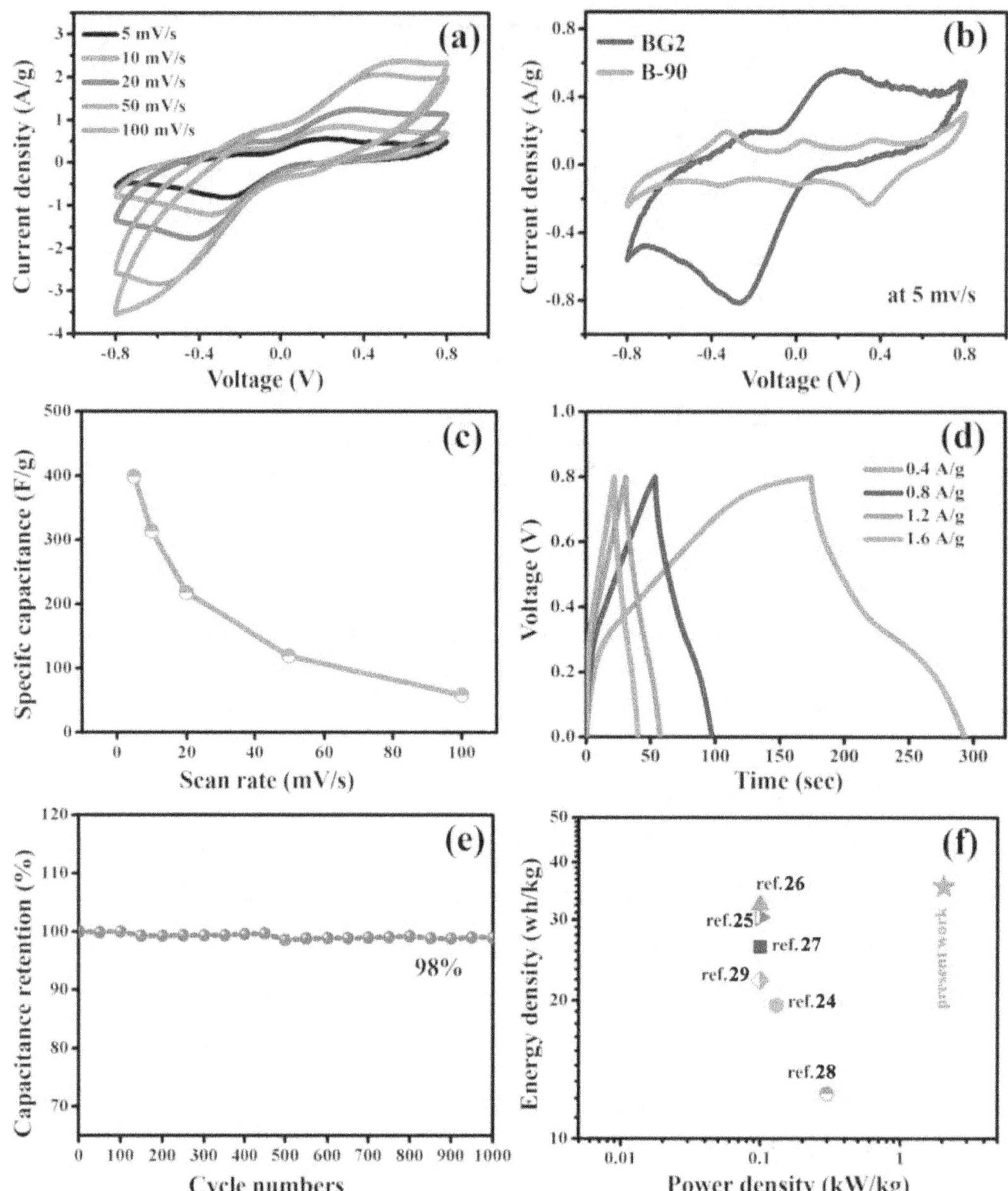

Figure 5.12: CV graph of (a) BG2 at different scan rates, (b) B-90 and BG2 at 5mV/s respectively, (c) scan rate vs specific capacitance graph of BG2, (d) galvanometric charging discharging graphs of BG2 at different current density, (e) cycle stability graph of BG2 (i) Ragone plot for $BiVO_4$/rGO hybrid (solid star) compared with the reported metal oxides.

Galvanometric charging discharging performance of the BG2 hybrid electrodes at different current density displayed typical pseudocapacitive nature and are shown in the Fig.5.12d. Cycling stability is an important parameter to determine the performance of the supercapacitor. As fabricated $BiVO_4$/rGO (BG2) symmetric supercapacitor shows excellent stability after 1000 cycles, displays in the Fig.5.12e. The BiVO$_4$/rGO (BG2) symmetric supercapacitor retains its 98% initial capacitance after 1000 cycles. The obtained energy density for hybrid electrode is 35.37 Wh/kg at power density 2.05kW/kg. The Ragone plot of the as prepared hybrid sample and the other metal oxides based solid state supercapacitors is represented in the Fig.5.12f. The observed specific energy density is higher than the previously reported solid state supercapacitors based on metal oxides. [24-29] We have also studied the electrochemical performances of the B-90 and BG2 samples using 1M Na$_2$SO$_4$ electrolyte (Fig.5.13) by two electrode system.

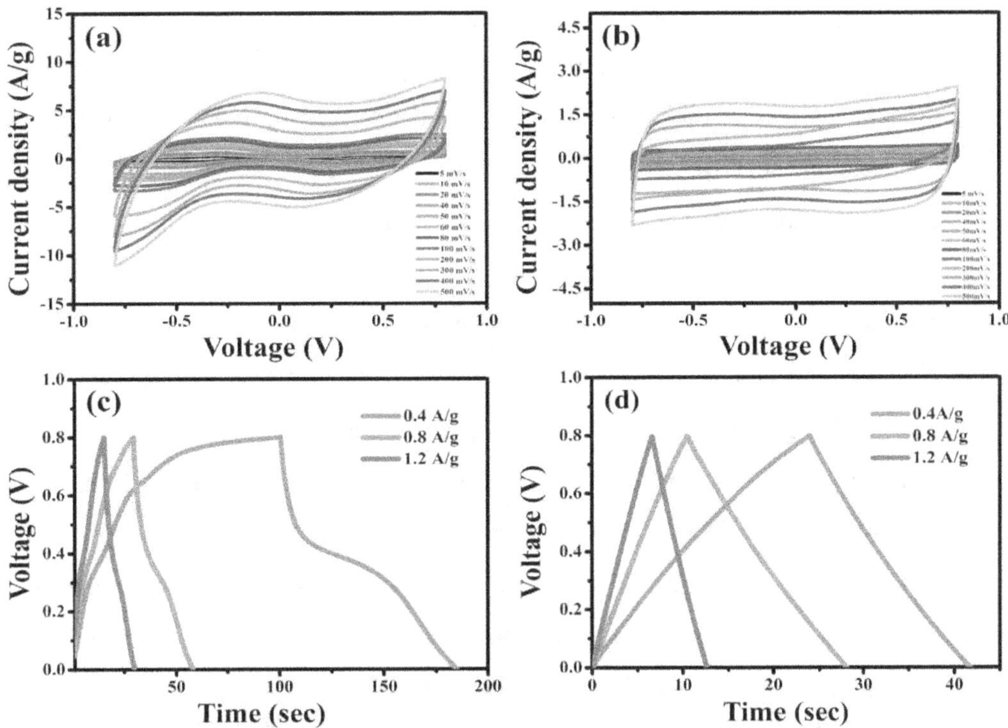

Figure 5.13: CV graphs of (a) BG2 and (b) B-90 at different scan rates and CD graphs of (c) BG-2 and (d) B-90 at different current density using 1M Na$_2$SO$_4$ electrolyte.

Fig.5.15(a) and (b) shows the cycling stability and FESEM micrographs of BG2 sample after 1000 cycle of CV execution using 1M Na$_2$SO$_4$ aqueous electrolyte exhibiting 93% of retention and durability of our sample respectively.

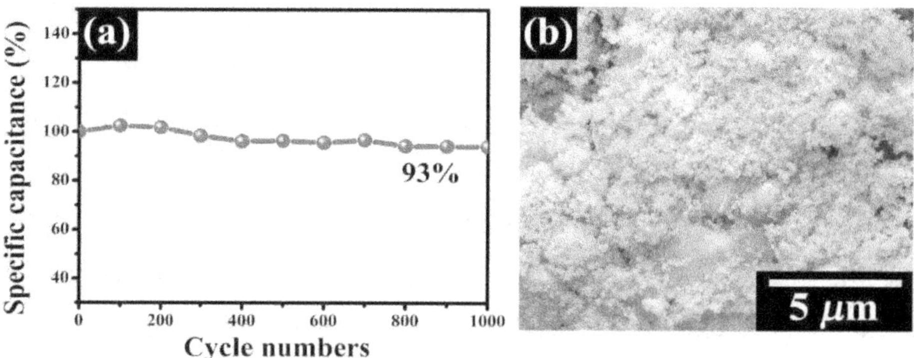

***Figure 5.14: Cycling stability of BG2 for 1000 cycles at a scan rate of 100 mV s^{-1}
using 1M Na$_2$SO$_4$ electrolyte, (b) FESEM image of BG2 sample after cycle test.***

The non-ideal rectangular nature of the CV curves is also obtained in 1M Na$_2$SO$_4$
neutral electrolyte, which indicates the pseudo capacitive behaviors of the electrodes.
The maximum specific capacitance value for BG2 electrode is 245 F/g at 5mV/s scan
rate, whereas that for B-90 electrode is 39 F/g at the same scan rate. The result clearly
shows better performance of the electrodes in presence of PVA/H$_2$SO$_4$ gel electrolyte.
The presence of –OH groups of PVA may absorbs large water contents and enhances
the ionic conductivity of the electrolyte as well as the electrochemical performances.

We have also performed the electrochemical impedance spectroscopy tests to evaluate
the capacitive nature of the supercapacitors. Fig. 5.15 (a) and (b) show the Nyquist plots
of the B-90 and BG2 electrodes using both 1M Na$_2$SO$_4$ and PVA/H$_2$SO$_4$ gel electrolyte
over the frequency range 0.1 Hz to 0.1MHz and 0.01 Hz to 0.1MHz respectively. The
equivalent series resistance values of the BG2 hybrid electrode in PVA/H$_2$SO$_4$ gel and
1M Na$_2$SO$_4$ electrolyte are obtained 2.8 and 3.8 ohm for respectively.

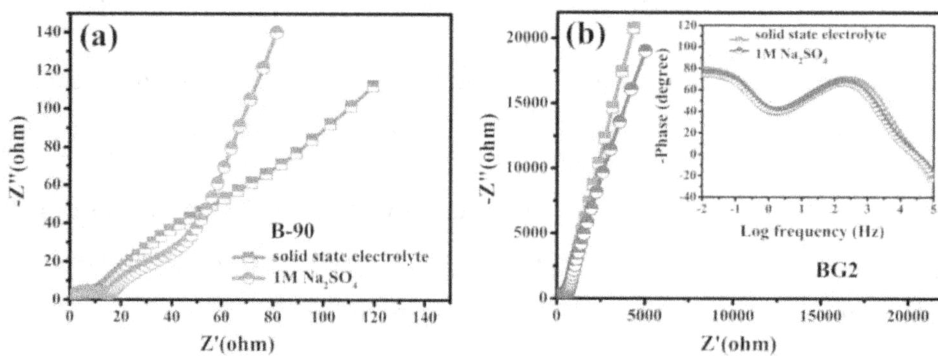

Figure 5.15: (a) Nyquist impedance plots for B-90 and (b) Nyquist impedance plots for
BG2; the inset shows bode plots.

Further the straight line at low frequency region in the Nyquist plot in presence of both the electrolyte is almost parallel to the imaginary axis, which indicates the ideal capacitive performance of the supercapacitor based on BG2 hybrid electrode. The phase angle of $BiVO_4/rGO$ electrodes at low frequency region for both the cases are closed to $80°$ (Fig.5.15b inset), which also indicates the high capacitive behavior of the electrode.

5.5 Summary

In summary, we have synthesized $BiVO_4$ embedded rGO hybrid nanostructure by a simple cost effective hydrothermal method. Structure, surface morphology and capacitive behaviors of $BiVO_4/rGO$ hybrid were well investigated. X-ray diffraction pattern indicates the formation of pure phase monoclinic structure of the $BiVO_4$. We have studied the electrochemical properties of as prepared hybrid to know its performance as symmetric supercapacitor electrodes with both PVA/H_2SO_4 solid and Na_2SO_4 aqueous electrolytes. The obtained maximum specific capacitance is 400 F/g at 5 mV/s scan rate in solid electrolyte and 245 F/g in aqueous Na_2SO_4 at same scan rate. High energy density (35.37 Wh/Kg) and excellent cycle stability makes this hybrid suitable for application in supercapacitor.

5.6 References

1) S .Arico, P. Bruce, B. Scrosati, J.M. Tarascon and W.V. Schalkwijk, *Nat. Mater.*, 2005, **4**, 366-377.

2) P .Simon and Y .Gogotsi , *Nat. Mater.*,2008, **7**, 845-854.

3) J. W. Lang, L B.Kong, W. J.Wu, Y. C. Luo and L.Kang, *Chem. Commun.*, 2008, 4213-4215.

4) N. R. Chodankar, D. P. Dubal, G. S Gund and C.D. Lokhande, *J. Energy Chem.*,2016 **25**, 463-471.

5) H. Kim and B. N. Popov, *J. Power Sources*, 2002, **104**, 52-61.

6) H. L.Wang, H.S. Casalongue ,Y.Y. Liang and H. J. Dai, *J. Am. Chem. Soc.*, 2010, **132**, 7472-7477.

7) P. Madhusudan, J. Ran, J. Zhang, J. Yu and G. Liu, *Appl. Catal.B*, 2011, **110**, 286–295.

8) H. Jiang, H. Endo, H. Natori, M. Nagai and K. Kobayashi, *Mater. Res. Bull.*, 2009, **44**, 700-706.

9) T. Lu and B.C.H. Steele, *Solid State Ionics*, 1986, **21**, 339-342.

10) L. Zhang, D. Chen and X. Jiao, *J. Phys.Chem. B*, 2006, **110**, 2668-2673.

11) H. Liu, R. Nakamura and Y. Nakato, *J. Electrochem.Soc*, 2005, **152**, G856-G861.

12) J. B. Liu, H. Wang, S. Wang and H. Yan, *Mater. Sci. Eng.B* ,2003, **104**, 36-39.

13) A. Galembeck and O. L. Alves, *Thin Solid Films* ,2000, **365**, 90-93.

14) Z. Khan, S. Bhattu, S. Haram and D. Khushalani , *RSC Adv.*,2014, **4**, 17378–1738.

15) S.S. Patil, D.P. Dubal, V.G.Deonikar, M.S Tamboli, J.D. Ambekar , P.Gomez-Romero, S.S. Kolekar, B. B. Kale and D. R .Patil, *ACS Appl. Mater. Interfaces,* 2016, **8**, 31602–31610.

16) Y.Arora, *Sci. Rep.*,2016, **6**, 36294.

17) W. S. Hummers and R. E. Offema, *J. Am. Chem. Soc.*,1957, **208**, 1937.

18) L. Zhang, D. Chen and X. Jiao, *J. Phys. Chem. B*, 2006, **110**, 2668-2673.

19) B. Liu, Z. Li, S. Xu, X. Ren, D. Han and D. Lu, *J. Phys. Chem. Solids*, 2014, **75**, 977–983.

20) J. K. Park, K.W. Lee, J.H. Han, J. J. Kweon, D.Kim, C. E. Lee, S .Lim, G. Kim, S.J. Noh and H.S.Kim, *J. Appl. Phys. ,*2013, **114**, 214310-214310-4.

21) X .Wu, J. Zhao, S. Guo, L. Wang, W. Shi, H. Huang, Y. Liu and Z. Kang, ***Nanoscale***, 2016 **8,** 17314-17321.

22) L. Zhang, D. Chen and X. Jiao, *J. Phys. Chem. B,* 2006, **110**, 2668-2673.

23) S.S. Patil, D.P. Dubal D, M.S. Tamboli, J.D. Ambekar , S. S. Kolekar, P. Gomez-Romero, B.B. Kale and D.R. Patil, *J. Mater.Chem. A*, 2016, **4**,7580-7584.

24) Q.T. Qu, L. Li, S. Tian, W. Guo, Y. P. Wu and R. Holze, *J. Power Sources,* 2010 ,**195** 2789-2794.

25) Z. S.Wu, W. Ren, D.W. Wang, F .Li , B. Liu and H. M .Cheng, *ACS Nano,* 2010,**4**, 5835-5842.

26) X. Zhao, L. Zhang, S. Murali, M. D. Stoller, Q. Zhang, Y.Zhu and R.S. Ruoff , *ACS Nano,* 2012, **6**, 5404-5412.

27) J. Zhang, J. H. Li and X. S. Zhao, *Energy Environ. Sci.*, 2011, **4**, 4009-4015.

28) Q. Wang, Z. Wen and J. H. Li, *Adv. Funct. Mater.,* 2006, **16**, 2141-2146.

29) Z. Lei, J. Zhang and X. S. Zhao, *J Mater.Chem.,* 2012, **22**, 153-160.

Chapter 6

Light-Weight Flexible Solid-State Supercapacitor Based on Highly Crystalline 2-D BiOCl Nanoplates/ MWCNT Nanocomposites

Work presented in this chapter has been published in:

J.Alloys Compd. 820 (2020) 153115

Shibsankar Dutta, Debopriya Shikder, Shreyasi Pal and Sukanta De

6.1. Introduction

Multi-electron transfer properties of Bismuth oxides and Bismuth oxyhalides during electrochemical reaction make them attractive candidates for supercapacitor application. Nano sheets, nano belts and different nano structures of bismuth oxides based supercapacitor were reported which exhibiting specific capacitances between 98~996 F/g. Bi_2O_3 film grown on copper substrates using electroplating as supercapacitor electrode was first reported by Gujar and his co-worker.[5] Asymmetric supercapacitor based on (+ electrode) MnO_2//(- electrode)β-Bi_2O_3 was reported by Ma et al , which obtained high energy density of 32.4Wh/ kg.[6] Bismuth oxychloride (BiOCl) another member of the same family have tetragonal lamellar structure, in which [Cl–Bi–O–Bi–Cl] sheets are stacked together by the van der Waals interaction through the Cl atoms along the c-axis. Until now, different morphologies of BiOCl materials by several synthesis procedures were reported.[7-13] Among different morphologies two-dimensional BiOCl nanoplate has shown potential applications in photocatalytic, optical, electrical and biomedical grounds because of its perfect crystallinity, geometric anisotropy, excellent photostability, electronic properties and nontoxicity. Wang et.al reported one-pot strategy for the synthesis of uniform PANi thorn/BiOCl chip (BPB) heterostructures at a low temperature using Bi_2S_3 nanowires and that BPB-modified electrode exhibited an specific capacitance of 169.9 F/ g at 0.5 A/ g. One dimensional polyaniline thorn/BiOCl chip heterostructures: self-sacrificial template-induced synthesis and electrochemical performance.[14] Liu and his co-worker reported AC/BiOCl asymmetric supercapacitor, exhibits a maximum capacitance value of 124 F/ g at 0.5 A/ g.[15] Q.X. Xia et al. reported a bismuth oxychloride nanosheets-immobilised $Ti_3C_2T_x$ MXene material (TCBOC) electrode with specific capacitance 247.8 F/g at the current density of 1 A/g.[16] Nevertheless, to the best of our knowledge, except these few reports there is no other report on BiOCl as supecapacitor electrode.

Here, we have adopted a simple, cost-effective hydrothermal approach for the synthesis of scalable amount of 2D bismuth oxychloride (BiOCl) nanoplates. Thin flexible films of BiOCl/MWCNT composites have been prepared with varying the weight percentage. A remarkable electrochemical performance has been obtained for BiOCl/MWCNT flexible solid state symmetric supercapacitor (FSSSC) with PVA/H_2SO_4 gel as solid electrolyte. Among various compositions, 60% BiOCl loaded electrodes ($FSSC_{60}$) delivers a highest specific capacitance of 421F/g at 5mV/s. Furthermore, $FSSSC_{60}$

exhibits a high energy density of 14.62 Wh/kg at power density 947.5 W/kg. The $FSSSC_{60}$ shows excellent durability with 94 % of initial specific capacitance after 2000 cycles. In addition, as fabricated device exhibits good flexibility and retains almost constant performance after bending through different angles.

6.2. Experimental

6.2.1.Materials:

Bismuth nitrate $[Bi(NO_3)_3 \cdot 5H_2O]$, potassium chloride (KCl) sodium hydroxide (NaOH), sodium dodecyl sulfate (SDS, >90%), sulphuric acid (H_2SO_4, 98%), polyvinyal alcohol (PVA) were purchased from Merck Specialties Pvt. Ltd. Multiwall carbon nanotube (OD: 60-100 nm, L: 5-15nm) was purchased from io-Il-Tech nanomateials. All chemicals were used without further purification.

6.2.2. Synthesis of BiOCl nano-plate:

The plate-like BiOCl was synthesized according to the procedure described in the previously reported literature.[17] In detail, 2 mmol of $Bi(NO_3)_3 \cdot 5H_2O$ and 2 mmol of KCl were successively dissolved into 30 mL of deionized water under magnetic stirring at room temperature, Subsequently, pH value of solution was adjusted to about 6.0 by adding 1M NaOH solution. After continuously stirring for 30 min, mixture solution was transferred into 50 mL Teflon-lined stainless steel autoclave and allowed to be heated at 160 °C for 24 h in a static state. After that allowed it to air cooled to room temperature. The resulting white particles were collected and successively washed with ethanol and deionized water and finally dried at 60 °C in air.

6.2.3. Preparation of CNT dispersions:

Firstly, stock solutions of sodium dodecylsulphate (SDS) of concentration 5mg/ml in deionized water was prepared by overnight magnetic stirring at room temperature. Subsequently, carbon nanotube dispersions were prepared using SDS solutions with surfactant, CNT mass ratio 5:1, under high power ultrasonic irradiation for 5 minutes followed by low power sonic bath treatment for 1 hour. Finally, dispersions were subjected for another 5 minutes high power ultrasonic irradiation treatment. After overnight rest, dispersions were centrifuged at 5500 rpm for 90 minutes. Lastly, for future application supernatant was carefully decanted.[18] We have followed this method to disperse both SWCNT and MWCNT.

6.2.4. Electrode preparation:

BiOCl nano-plates of concentration 1mg/ml were dispersed in ethanol by low power ultrasonic bath sonication for 5 minutes. Subsequently, prepared MWCNT dispersions and BiOCl dispersions were mixed together with different weight percentages to make thin films on cellulose membranes with masking one portion using vacuum filtration. After complete filtration, the film was allowed to dry on filter membrane keeping the filtration setup intact. We have removed the mask before depositing SWCNT thin film on top of BiOCl/MWCNT film under vacuum filtration condition and washed with DI water several times (as shown in the fig.1). Then thin films were transfer on flexible PET substrate as reported in the literature.[19]

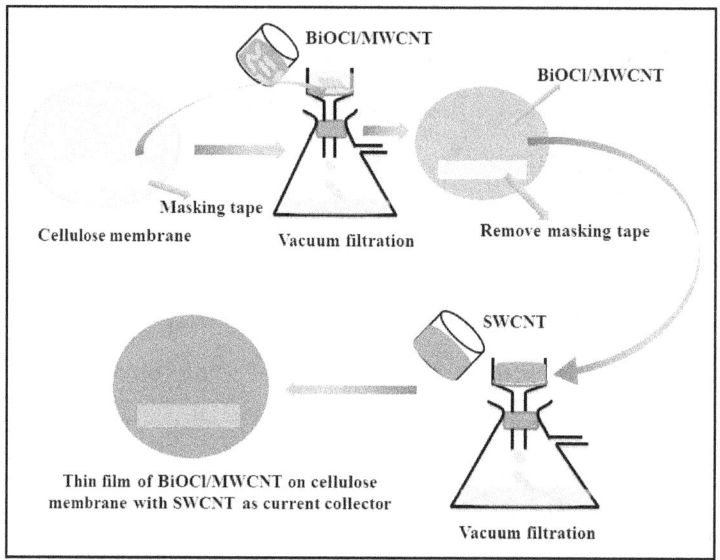

Figure 6.1. Thin film Preparation using vacuum filtration

6.2.5. Fabrication of flexible symmetric solid state supercapacitor (FSSSC):

BiOCl/MWCNT thin films on flexible PET substrates were used as both positive and negative electrode, whereas PVA/H_2SO_4 gel sandwiched between the electrodes acted as solid electrolyte of FSSSC (fig.6.2) where SWCNT network in between PET and composite thin film act as current collectors. Henceforth, We designate the solid state supercapacitors with loading 100 wt%, 75 wt%, 60 wt %, 50 wt %, 25 wt % and 0 wt% BiOCl as $FSSSC_{100}$, $FSSSC_{75}$, $FSSSC_{60}$, $FSSSC_{50}$, $FSSSC_{25}$ and $FSSSC_0$ respectively.

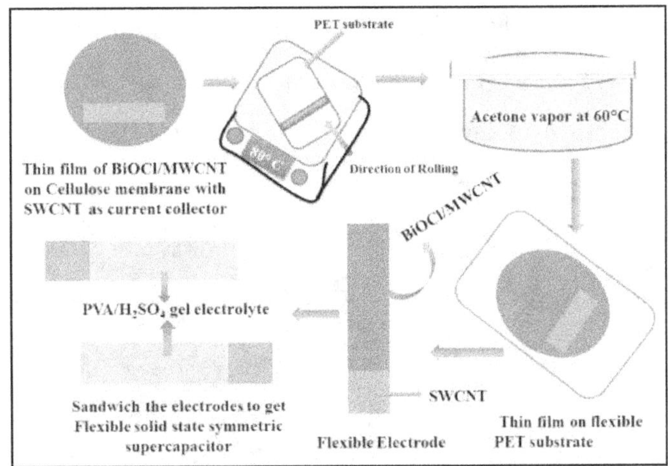

Figure 6.2. Fabrication of Flexible solid state supercapacitor

5.3. Characterization

Scanning electron microscope (SEM) images were taken by a FEI, MERLIN (Carl Zeiss) Scanning Electron Microscope. The Brunauer–Emmett–Teller (BET) and pore size distribution of samples were determined by Autosorb iQ Station 1 instrument using liquid nitrogen at 77 K based on the nitrogen adsorption-desorption isotherm. Transmission electron microscope (TEM) images of BiOCl were taken by JEM 2100 at an accelerating voltage of 200 keV. The structure of BiOCl and composite were examined by Rigaku-Ultima III X-ray diffractometer with CuKα radiation ($l = 1.5418$ Å) X-ray diffraction (XRD-6000) with Cu Kα radiation operating at 40kV, 60mA. Raman spectra were done with IHR550 spectrometer and a laser excitation wavelength of 532 nm. The electrochemical performance of BiOCl nano-plate and BiOCl/MWCNT were measured using two electrode system operated at CHI660E electrochemical work station at room temperature. Cyclic voltammetry (CV) and galvanometric charging discharging (GCD) tests of supercapacitors were measured with the potential window 0V to 1V. Electrochemical impedance spectroscopies (EIS) of the electrodes were recorded between 0.01 Hz to 100 KHz.

6.4. Result and discussion

6.4.1. Structural & morphological analysis:

Plate-like morphology of as prepared BiOCl were observed under transmission electron microscopy (TEM) image shown in Figure 6.3a. The selected-area electron diffraction (SAED) pattern (inset of Fig.6.3c) corresponding to the nano plates indicated the single-crystalline nature. Notably the size of the obtained nano-plate is about 500 nm as shown in the fig 6.3(b). High-resolution TEM (HRTEM) image (Figure 6.3b) displays clear and continuous lattice fringes having lattice spacing of 0.275nm along the (110) atomic planes respectively.[15,17] The selected-area electron diffraction (SAED) pattern of the nano-plate is shown in the inset of fig.6.3c and revels the angle between (110) and (200) plane is 45° which is well match to the theoretical value.[17]

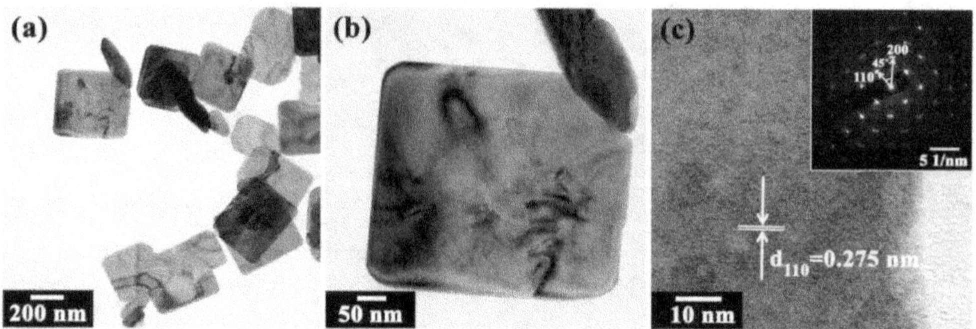

Figure.6.3 (a) TEM image of the BiOCl nanoplates (BC100:0), (b) TEM image of single BC100:0 nanoplate surface, (c) HRTEM image of the BC100:0 nanoplate surface and insert is the corresponding SAED pattern.

Fig 6.4(a) represent the schematic illustration of the crystal orientation of the BiOCl nanoplate whereas fig.6.4(b) shows the side and top view of the crystal structure.Fig.6.4(c) depicts the EDAX spectrum of BiOCl nanoplates conforming the presence Bi, O and Cl elements and their atomic % values are present in the table of fig.6.4(d) which indicates the atomic percentage ratio of Bi:O is 0.96 and O:Cl is 1.01 which are very close to 1.

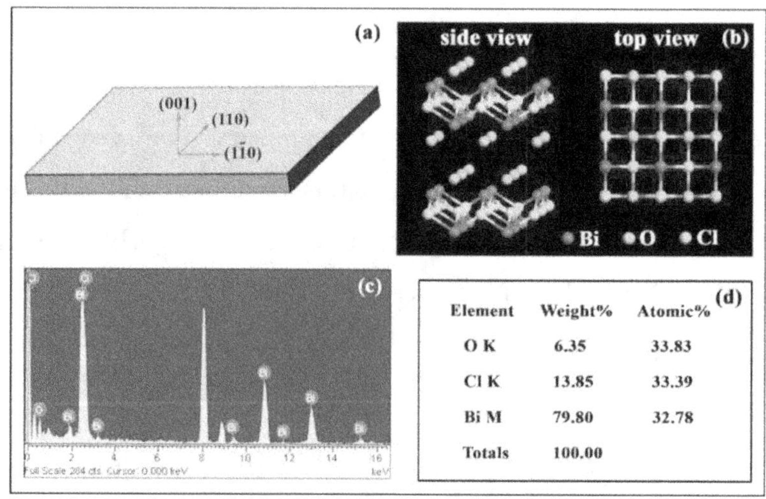

Element	Weight%	Atomic%
O K	6.35	33.83
Cl K	13.85	33.39
Bi M	79.80	32.78
Totals	100.00	

Figure.6.4. (*a***) Schematic illustration of the crystal orientation of the BiOCl nanoplate. (f) the crystal structure of BiOCl of the {001} facets; (c,d) EDX spectrum and corresponding atomic percentages of the BiOCl nanoplates (BC100:0).

The FESEM images reveals that the prepared samples consisted with 2 dimensional plate-like structures having size ~200-500 nm and thicknesses of 10-20 nm (Fig.6.5). The Fig 6.5(a-f) represents the FESEM images of the BiOCl/MWCNT composite thin films with different loading weight percentages of (100:0), (75:25), (60:40), (50:50), (25:75) and (0:100) respectively. we designate the samples corresponding to 100 Wt% of BiOCl, 75 Wt% of BiOCl, 60 Wt% of BiOCl, 50 Wt% of BiOCl, 25 Wt% of BiOCl and 0% of BiOCl as BC(100:0), BC(75:25), BC(60:40), BC(50:50), BC(25:75) and BC(0:100) respectively. The composite thin films exhibited an interconnected porous network, where MWCNTs were played the roles of the structural scaffolds. Further it is clearly visible that the most porous network was obtained for the (60:40) BiOCl/MWCNT composite, which explore more electro-active sites to the electrolyte ions and used for electrochemical studies.

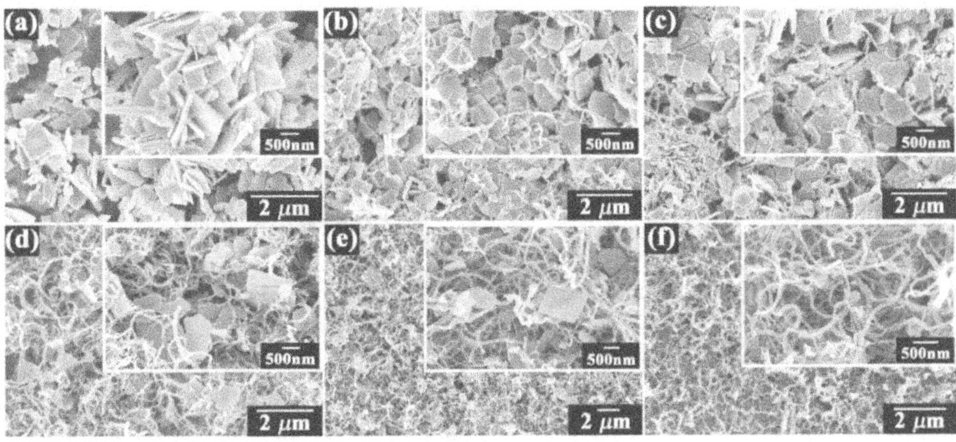

Figure.6.5. FESEM images of BiOCl nanoplates and BiOCl/MWCNT nanocomposites (a) BC100:0, (b) BC75:25, (c) BC60:40, (d) BC50:50, (e) BC25:75 and (f) BC0:100 respectively, Insets showing their high magnification images.

The crystallographic natures of the prepared samples were characterized by X-ray diffraction (XRD). Fig.6.6(a,(i)) shows the XRD pattern of the obtained BiOCl samples in the 2θ range from 10° to 80°. The observed diffraction peaks of the sample at 12°, 24°, 26°, 32°, 33°, 35°, 36°, 41°, 47°, 48°, 50°, 53°, 54°, 55°, 58°, 60°, 67°, 68°, 70°, 72°, 75°, 78° are assigned to the (001), (002), (101), (110), (102), (111), (003), (112), (200), (201), (113), (202), (211), (104), (212), (114), (220), (221), (204), (115), (214), (310) planes, which is well matched the reference BiOCl crystal structure (JCPDS No.06-0249). [15] The high diffraction peak ratio value of (101), (102) and (110) planes over the (001) plane suggests that the sample is preferentially grown along the

(101), (102), and (110) directions. Further no other impurity related peaks confirms the phase purity as well as the highly crystalline nature of the as-synthesized BiOCl samples. The XRD pattern of BiOCl/MWCNT (60:40) thin film (Fig.6.6 (a, ii) reveals that the diffraction peaks for MWCNT at 25.8° related to (002) plane overlapped with the peaks of BiOCl corresponding to 101 plane at 26°. All other diffraction peaks of BiOCl are presents in the XRD patterns of the composite.

Fig. 6.6(b) shows the Raman spectra of the sample. The peaks at 141 cm^{-1} is due the A1g stretching vibration of Bi-Cl. The peaks at 197 cm^{-1} is also assigned to the stretching vibration of Bi-Cl whereas peak at 396 cm^{-1} is attributed to the stretching vibration of Bi-O. [23,24] The Raman spectra of the composite(60wt% BiOCl and 40wt % of MWCNT) thin film depicts D and G peaks of MWCNT as well as peaks corresponding to BiOCl,[25] which conforms the presence of both MWCNT and BiOCl in the thin films, as shown in the Fig. 6.6(c).

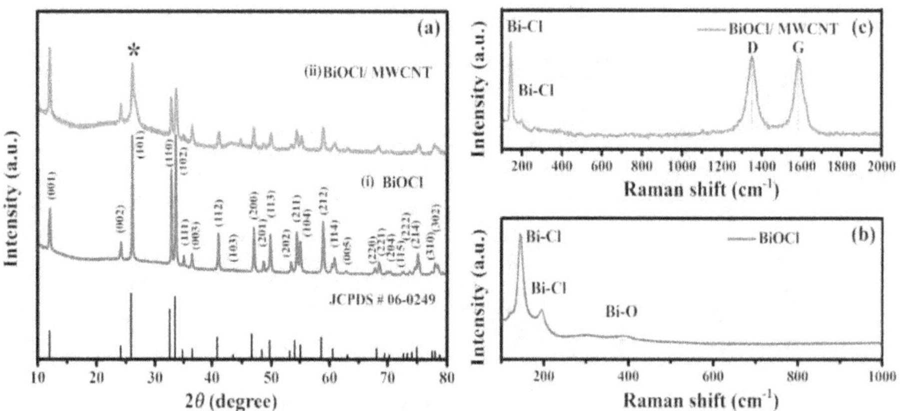

Figure.6.6. (a) XRD patterns and (b,c) Raman spectra of the BiOCl nanoplates (BC100:0) and BC60:40 BiOCl/MWCNT composites.

The chemical compositions and surface electronic state of the prepared BiOCl was investigated by X-ray photoelectron spectroscopy (XPS). The survey XPS Spectrum (Fig.6.7a) indicates the presence of Bi, O, Cl and C only. The signal at 284.48 eV is assigned to C1s, (Fig. 6.7b) which comes from the hydrocarbon of the XPS instrument itself.[26]. The two strong peaks at 165.2 eV (Bi4f5/2) and 159.9 eV (Bi4f7/2) in the Bi4f spectrum (Fig. 6.7c) are observed which indexed to the Bi^{3+} in BiOCl.[27,28] The peaks at 198.4 (Cl2p3/2) and 200 eV(Cl2p1/2) displayed in the Fig. 6.7d is the characteristic of Cl in BiOCl.[29] On the other hand the peak at 530.5 eV shown in the Fig. 6.7e was assigned to O1s of BiOCl.

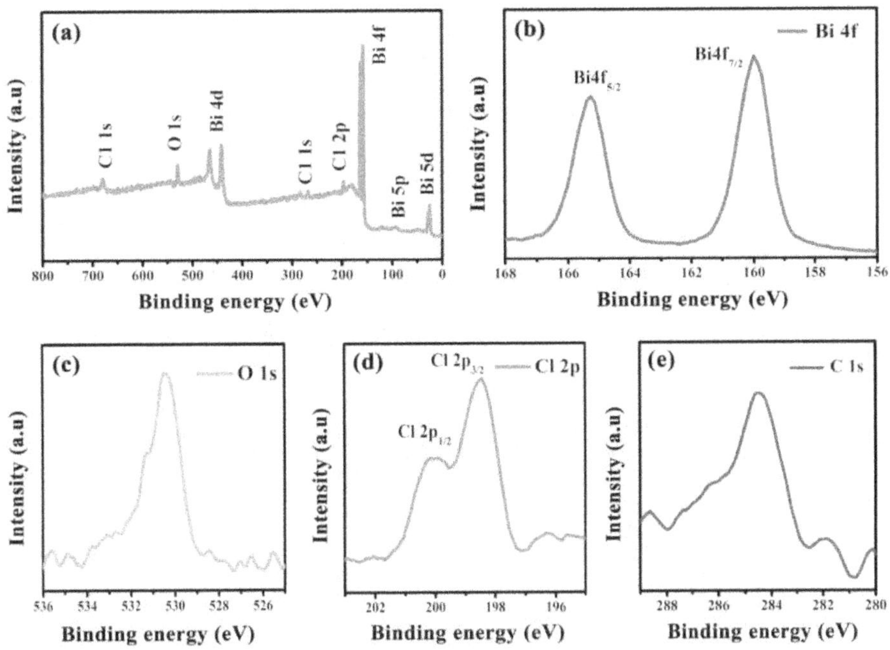

Figure 6.7. (a) XPS survey scan and XPS spectrum of the (b) Bi 4f, (c) O1s, (d) Cl 2p and (e) C 1s of the BC100:0 samples.

The N_2 adsorption–desorption measurement of the samples were done to obtain the textural parameters. The N_2 adsorption/desorption isotherms and corresponding pore size distribution curves (inset) of all the samples were shown in the figure 6.8(a)-(f). It can be observed that isotherms are of type-IV according to the IUPAC nomenclature and exhibit H3 hysteresis, which implies a mesoporous nature of the samples.[15]The specific surface area and pore size of the samples are presented in the table 6.1. From the bar diagram (Fig.6.9) it is evident that among the all sample BiOCl/ MWCNT (60/40) delivered more specific surface area as well as more pore volume and these results matching our FESEM results.

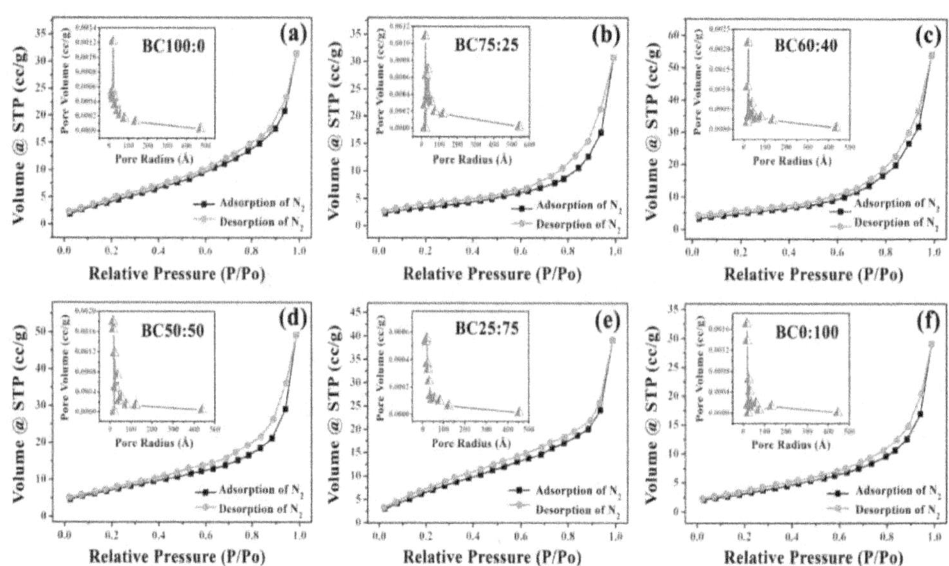

Figure 6.8. N_2 adsorption–desorption isotherms and corresponding BJH pore size distribution plots (inset fig) (a) BC100:0, (b) BC75:25, (c) BC60:40, (d) BC50:50, (e) BC25:75 and (f) BC0:100 respectively

Table 6.1. Textural parameters from BET analysis

Electrode Samples	Specific Surface Area (m²/g)	Pore radius (Å)	Pore Volume (cc/g)
BC100	15.139	20.408	0.047
BC75	15.668	20.606	0.051
BC60	22.750	20.332	0.072
BC50	22.099	16.229	0.061
BC25	19.824	20.023	0.059
BC0	15.268	16.289	0.034

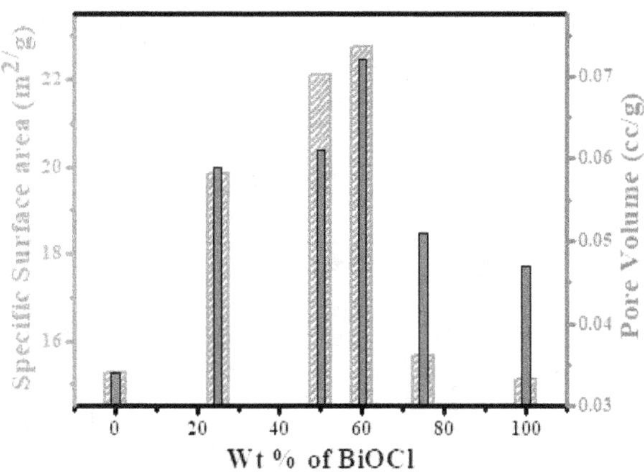

Figure6.9. Specific surface areas and pore volumes of all the samples from BET analysis. Specific surface areas and pore volumes of all the samples from BET analysis.

6.4.2. Electrochemical tests of the symmetric supercapacitor:

To investigate the electrochemical performance of the as-fabricated FSSSC device with different wt% of BiOCl/MWCNT loading, CV and GCD tests were carried out with potential window 0 V to 1 V at different scan rates and current densities respectively (Fig. 6.10 and 6.11).

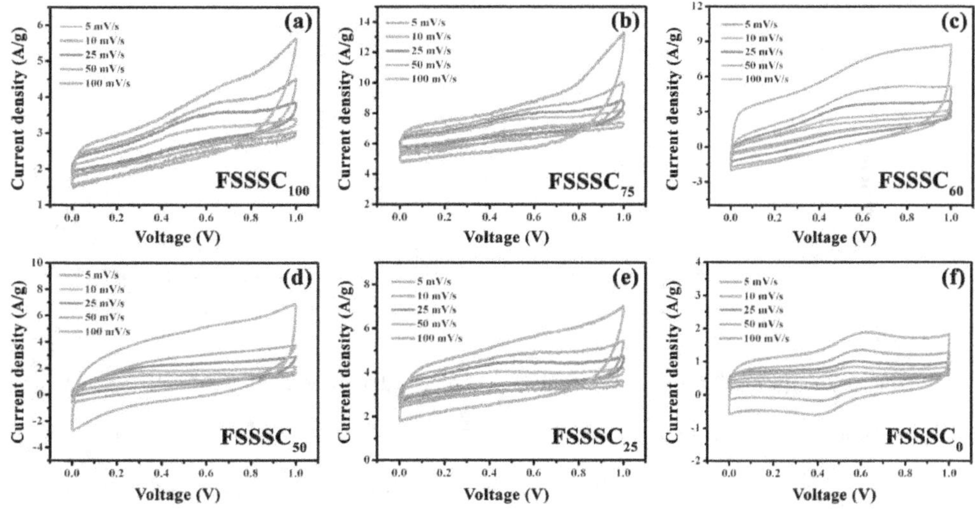

Figure 6.10. Cyclic voltammetry (CV) curves at different scan rates of (a) $FSSSC_{100}$, (b) $FSSSC_{75}$, (c) $FSSSC_{60}$, (d) $FSSSC_{50}$, (e) $FSSSC_{25}$ and (f) $FSSSC_0$ devices respectively.

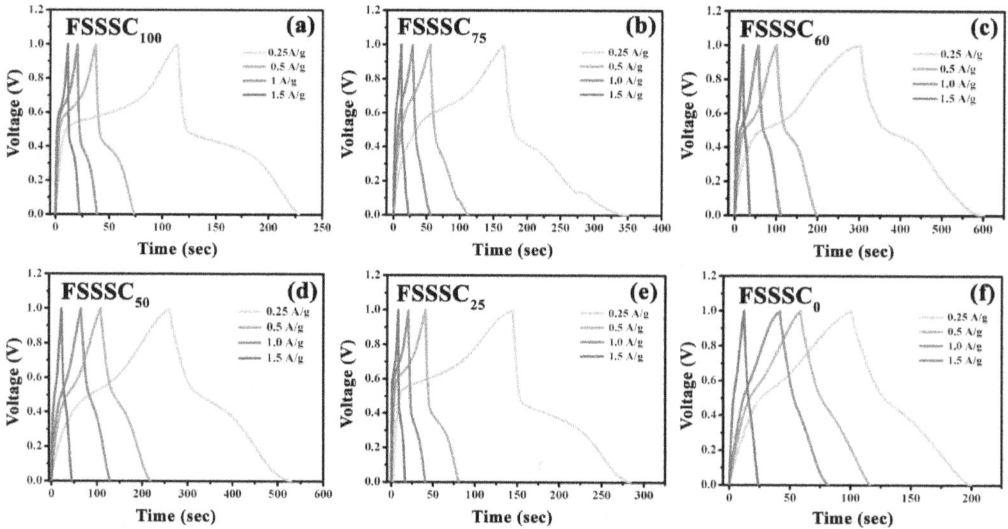

Figure 6.11. Galvanostatic charge discharge (GCD) curves at different current densities of SSC$_{100}$ (a), SSC$_{75}$ (b), SSC$_{60}$ (c), SSC$_{50}$ (d), SSC$_{25}$ (e) and SSC$_0$ (f) devices respectively.

Fig 6.12(a) displays the GCD curves of all the FSSSC devices at current density 0.25 A/g, where the FSSSC$_{60}$ (60:40 BiOCl/MWCNT composite) gives the highest specific capacitance values. The specific capacitance values at 0.25A/g current density of the all FSSSC devices are calculated and the corresponding graph is shown in Fig 6.12b.

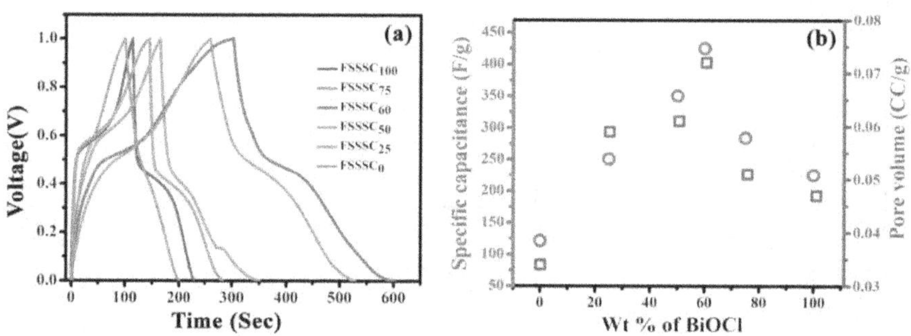

Figure 6.12. (a) GCD curves at a 0.25 A/g current density of all FSSSC (b) Specific capacitance and pore volume vs different wt% of BiOCl/MWCNT nano composites.

The superior electrochemical performance of FSSSC$_{60}$ amongst other different SSC can be attributed due to the best textural parameters (22.750 m^2/g surface area and 0.072 cc/g pore volume), obtained by BET analysis. The porous structure promotes electrolyte access and exposure the electro-active sites to the electrolyte. Also the conducting nature of MWCNT controls the fast charge transport. Thus we have picked 60:40(BiOCl/ MWCNT) composite electrode material for further electrochemical studies.

For further electrochemical study we have choose $FSSSC_{60}$ device. Fig.6.13 (a) and (b) shows the CV and GCD curves of $FSSSC_{60}$ at different scan rates and current density respectively. The obtained specific capacitance values from CV are 421F/g, 375 F/g, 323 F/g, 283 F/g, and 241 F/g at 5mv/s, 10 mV/s, 25 mV/s, 50 mV/s and 100 mV/s respectively. The redox reaction of H^+ ions with BiOCl can be described by the following reaction:

$$BiOCl + H_2O + 3e^- \rightarrow Bi + Cl^- + 2OH^-$$

$$2Bi + 6OH^- \leftrightarrow Bi_2O_3 + 3H_2O + 6e^-$$

Further we have measured the CV of $FSSSC_{60}$ by varying the voltage window for a fixed scan rate (100 mV/s) as shown in the fig.6.13(c). The CV curves maintain same nature at different potential windows, which indicates the stability of the supercapacitor. $FSSSC_{60}$ supercapacitor also shows outstanding stability after 2000 cycles, shown in the fig.6.13(d). The $FSSSC_{60}$ supercapacitor retains its 94% initial capacitance after 2000 cycles. The $FSSSC_{60}$ supercapacitor exhibits high energy density 14.62 Wh/kg at power density 947.5 W/kg. The Ragone plot of the as prepared $FSSSC_{60}$ and the previously reported symmetric and asymmetric supercapacitors is displayed in the Fig. 6.13(e).[15, 16, 30-37] We also studied electrochemical impedance spectroscopy tests to evaluate the capacitive behaviour of FSSSC60 Supercapacitor systematically. Fig. 6.13(f) shows Nyquist plots of electrodes over the frequency range of 0.01Hz 100 kHz. The corresponding equivalent circuit is shown in lower inset of Fig 6.13(e), which consists of a series and parallel combination of resistances, Rs, Rct (charge transfer resistance), CPE (constant phase element), and Zw (Warburg impedance).[35] The equivalent series resistance (ESR) values (Rs) is 3.94 Ω for SSC60. At lower frequency region in the Nyquist plot, the greater slope of the straight line indicates good capacitive behaviour of the sample, which also be conformed from the bode plot upper inset of Fig.6.13(e) where low frequency region phase angle closer to 65°.

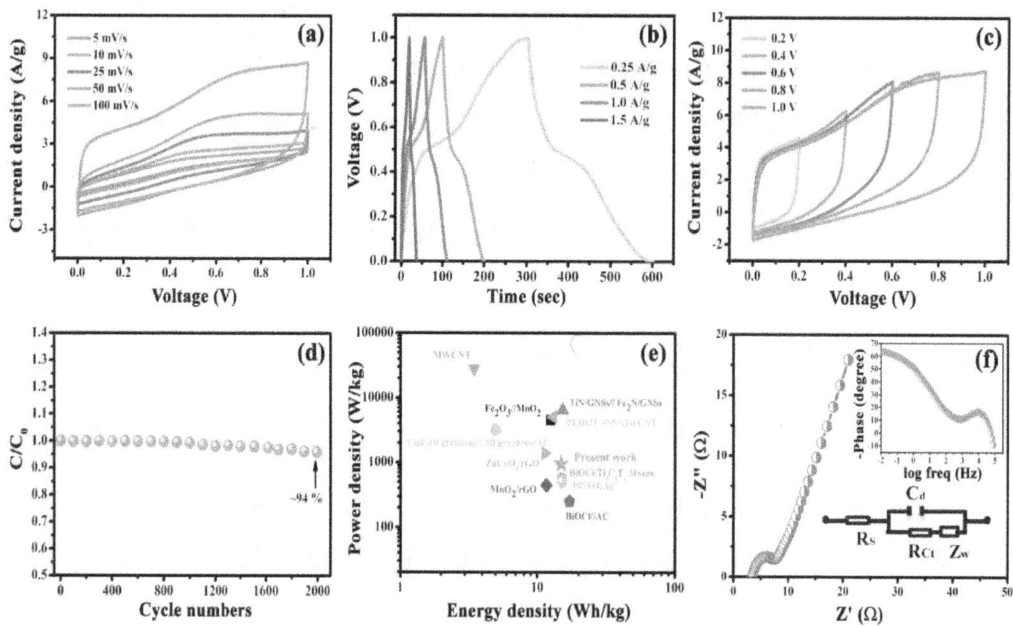

***Figure 6.13*.**(a) CV curves of FSSSC$_{60}$ at different scan rates.(b) GCD curves of FSSSC$_{60}$ at different current densities, (c) CV curves of FSSSC$_{60}$ at 100mV/s scan rate for different voltage windows,(d)Cycle stability curve of FSSSC$_{60}$ at 100 mV/s, (e) Ragone plot for FSSSC$_{60}$, (e) Nyquist plots of FSSSC$_{60}$ and lower and upper inset shows equivalent circuit, and Bode plot of FSSSC$_{60}$ respectively.

Flexibility is fast becoming an exclusive feature in modern electronic devices. To this end, we have investigated the performance of our devices under a variety of bending conditions. We have done cyclic voltammetry study (at 100 mV/s) for the device FSSSC$_{60}$ at different bending angle and no significant changes in CV curves were observed as shown in the fig.6.14 (a) and schematic of bending angle is shown in inset of fig. 12(a). The corresponding specific capacitance value was almost remaining same during different bending angle, which is displayed in the fig 6.14(b), inset of the fig 6.14(b) displayed flexible thin film of BiOCl/MWCNT on a PET substrate.

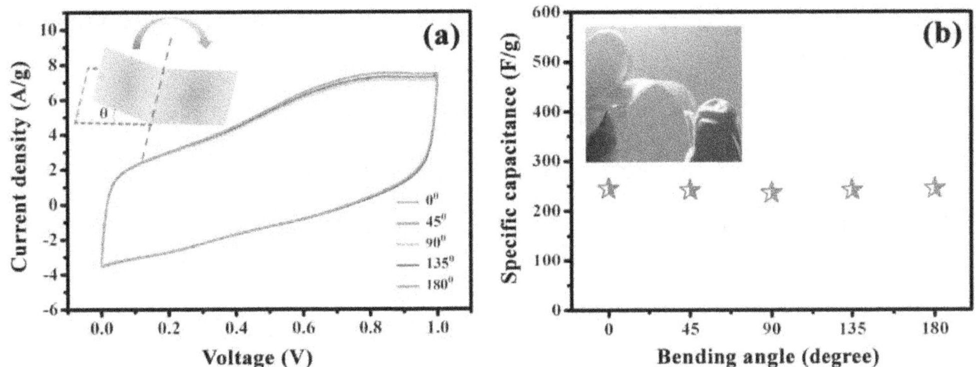

Figure 6.14.(a) Cyclic voltammetry curves at different bending conditions for FSSSC$_{60}$ at 100 mv/s scan rate, inset shows schematic diagram of bending angle, (b) Specific capacitance vs bending angle graph of FSSSC$_{60}$ and flexible electrode(inset fig).

6.5 Summary

In summary, we have fabricated 2D-BiOCl nanoplates / MWCNT nanocomposites based thin flexible supercapacitor with high specific capacitance and energy density and have been reported for the first time. Among different compositions, composite with 60 wt% exhibits highest specific capacitance of 421F/g and energy density 14.62 Wh/Kg. Variation in the electrochemical performance of BiOCl/MWCNT composites with different wt% is perfectly correlated with specific surface area and the pore size of composites. Excellent cycle stability with only 6% reduction in specific capacitance after 2000 cycles and good stability under bending, making the fabricated supercapacitor extremely promising as a flexible energy storage device.

6.6 References

1) L. Li, Z. A. Hu, N. An, Y. Y. Yang, Z. M. Li and H. Y. Wu, *J. Phys. Chem. C.* 2014, **118**, 22865-22872.

2) J. Jiang, Y. Li, J. Liu, X. Huang, C. Yuan and X. W. Lou, *Adv.Mater.* 2012, **24**, 5166–5180.

3) I.K. Chakraborty, N. Chakrabarty, A. Senapati and A.K. Chakraborty, *J.Phys. Chem. C* 2018, **122**, 27180-27190.

4) S. Pal, S. Majumder, S. Dutta, S. Banerjee, B. Satpati and S. De, *J. Phys. D: Appl. Phys.* 2018, **51**, 375501.

5) P. Gujar, V.R. Shinde, C.D. Lokhande and S.H. Han, *J. Power Sources.* 2006, **161**, 1479–1485.

6) X.J. Ma, W.B. Zhang, L.B. Kong, Y.C. Luo and L. Kang, *Electrochim. Acta.* 2016, **192**, 45–51.

7) S. Jiang, X. Peng, Y. Hu and Z. Gui, *Mater. Lett.* 2015, **161**, 561–564.

8) L. Ding, R. Wei, H. Chen, J. Hu, J. Li, *Appl. Catal. B Environ.* 2015, **172**, 91–99.

9) X. Gao, X. Zhang, Y. Wang, S. Peng, B. Yue and C. Fan, *Chem. Eng. J.* 2015, **263**, 419–426.

10) T. Li, L. Lin, H. Wei, G. Liang, X. Kuang and T. Liu, *Phys. E: Low-Dimensional Syst. Nanostructures.* 2016, **76**, 198–202.

11) X. Zhang, X. Liu, C. Fan, Y. Wang, W. Yunfang and Z. Liang, *Appl. Catal. B Environ.* 2013, **132**, 332–341.

12) Y. Wang, Z.Q. Shi, C.M. Fan, X.G. Hao, G.Y. Ding and Y.F. Wang, *Int. J. Miner. Metall. Mater.* 2012, **19**, 467–472.

13) D.H. Wang, G.Q. Gao, Y.W. Zhang, L.S. Zhou, A.W. Xu and W. Chen, *Nanoscale.* 2012, **4**, 7780-7785.

14) G. Nie, X. Lu, W. Wang, M. Chi, Y. Jiang and Ce. Wang, *Mater. Chem. Front.* 2017, **1**, 859-866.

15) W. Hong, L. Wang, K. Liu, X. Han, Y. Zhou, P. Gao, R. Ding and E. Liu, *J. Alloys Compd.* 2018, **746**, 292-300.

16) Q.X. Xia, N. Shinde, J.M.Yun, T. Zhang, R.S. Mane, Mathur and K.H. Skim, *Electrochim. Acta.* 2018, **271**, 351-360.

17) J. Jiang, K. Zhao, X. Xiao and L. Zhang,. *J. Am. Chem. Soc.* 2012, **134**, 4473-4476.

18) E.M. Doherty, S. De, P.E. Lyons, A. Shmeliov, P.N. Nirmalraj, V. Scardaci. J. Joimel, W.J. Blau, J.J. Boland and J.N. Coleman, *Carbon.* 2009, **47**, 2466-2473.

19) Z.C. Wu, Z.H. Chen, X. Du, J.M. Logan, J. Sippel and M. Nikolou. et al. *Science.* 2004, **305**, 1273–6.

20) K. Zhou, W. Zhou, X. Liu, Y. Sang, S. Ji, W. Li, J. Lu, L. Li, W. Niu, H. Liu and S. Chen, *Nano Energy.* 2015, **12**, 510-520.

21) H. Wang, H. Yi, X. Chen and X.Wang, *J. Mater. Chem. A* 2014, **2**, 3223-3230.

22) S. Ratha and C. S. Rout, *RSC Adv.* 2015, **5**, 86551-86557.

23) W. G. Fateley, N. T. Mcdecitt and F. F. Bentley, *Appl. Spectrosc.* 1971, **25**, 155.

24) V Tian, C. F. Guo, Y. J. Guo, Q. Wang and Q. Liu, *Appl. Surf. Sci.* 2012, **258**, 1949.

25) H. Qi, J. Liu and E. Mader, *Fibers.* 2014, **2**, 295-307.

26) J. Hu, W. Fan, W. Ye, C. Huang and X. Qiu, *Appl. Catal. B Environ.* 2014, **158**, 182–189.

27) H.Y. Jiang, K. Cheng and J. Lin, *Phys. Chem. Chem. Phys.* 2012, **14**, 12114–12121.

28) L. Ye, K. Deng, F. Xu, L. Tian, T. Peng and L. Zan, *Phys. Chem. Chem. Phys.* **2012**, *14*, 82–85.

29) C. Wang, C. Shao, Y. Liu and L. Zhang, *Scr. Mater.* 2008, **59**, 332–335.

30) L. Song, X. Cao, L. Li, Q. Wang, H, Ye, L. Gu, C. Mao, J. Song, S. Zhang and H. Niu, *Adv. Funct. Mater.*, 2017,**27**,1700474.

31) Z. Zhang, Q.C. Zheng and L. Sun, *Ceram Int.* 2017, **43**, 16217-16224.

32) C. Zhu, P. Yang, D. Chao, X. Wang, X. Zhang, S. Chen, B. K. Tay, H. Huang, H. Zhang, W. Mai and H. J. Fan, *Adv. Mater.*, 2015, **27**, 4566–4571

33) Z. Tian, H. Dou, B. Zhang, W. Fan and X. Wang, *Electrochim. Acta.* 2017, **237**, 109–118.

34) I. Moon, S. Yoon and J. Oh, *Chem.Eur. J.*, 2017, **23**, 597–604.

35) D. Zhao, Q. Zhang, W. Chen, X. Yi, S. Liu, Q. Wang, Y. Liu, J. Li, X. Li and H. Yu, *ACS Appl. Mater. Interfaces*, 2017, **9**, 13213–13222.

36) C. Zhu, P. Yang, D. Chao, X. Wang, X. Zhang, S. Chen, B. K. Tay, H. Huang, H. Zhang, W. Mai and H. J. Fan, *Adv. Mater.*, 2015, **27**, 4566–4571.

37) X. Li, K. Liu, Z. Liu, Z. Wang, B. Lia and D. Zhang, *Electrochim. Acta.* 2017, **240**, 43–52.

Chapter 7

MoS₂ Nanosheets/rGO Hybrid: An Electrode Material for High Performance Thin Film Supercapacitor

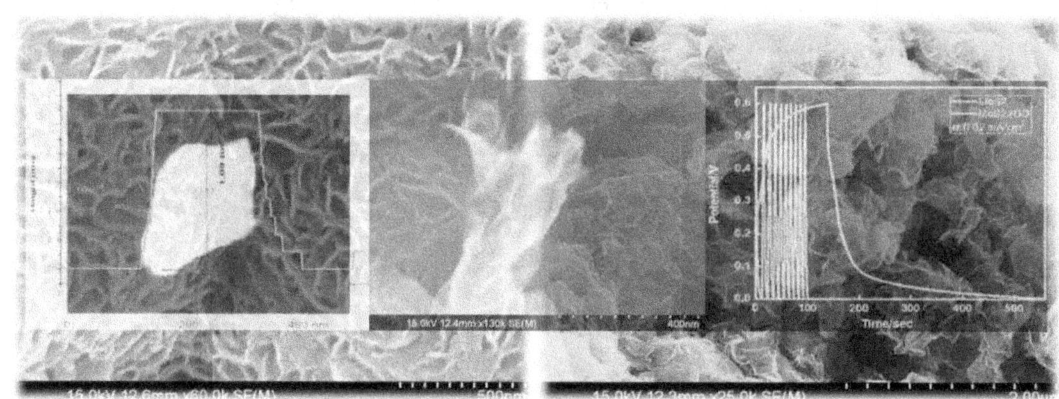

Work presented in this chapter has been published in:

Mater. Today Proc., 2018, 5, 9771–5

Shibsankar Dutta, Sukanta De.

7.1. Introduction

The growing demand for portable electronic has greatly promoted the development of thin film energy storage devices. It has been already reported that Graphene based supercapacitor obtained high volumetric capacitances of 300 F cm$^-$3.[1,2] Now a day this high values micro capacitors plays a crucial role for the development of the portable electronic technology. Atomic layer thickness and flat morphology of graphene analogues 2-D materials, such as transition metal dichalcogenides (MoS_2, $MoSe_2$, VS_2, and VSe_2 etc.) makes them promising candidates for thin film supercapacitor application. Unique structural (S-Mo-S) and electronic properties of MoS_2 nanosheets provide high specific surface area as well as due to the van der Waals forces between their layers, shows excellent intercalation of ions in layered MoS_2, which are the basic requirements for the high performance supercapacitor. [6-12] Several oxidation states from +2 to +6 of Mo centre in MoS_2 makes it a suitable candidate for pseudocapacitance. Graphene/MoS_2 [13] and polyaniline/MoS_2[14] hybrid electrodes have been already investigated as a supercapacitor.

We reported large scale production of MoS_2 and MoS_2/rGO hybrid by simple hydrothermal route followed by liquid phase exfoliation to get the nanosheets of the prepared sample.Electrochemical properties of hybrid electrode have been investigated systematically in 1M H_2SO_4 aqueous electrolyte using three electrode systems.

7.2. Experimental

7.2.1. Synthesis of MoS_2 and MoS_2/rGO

Bulk MoS_2 was prepared by simple hydrothermal route. 20 mmol MoO_3, 50 mmol potassium thiocyanate and 128 mg SDS (sodium dodecyl sulfate) were dispersed in 60 ml DI water using tip sonicator for 30 minutes and kept in 100 ml teflon coated autoclave at 220ºC for 24 hours. After cooling naturally the product was washed by centrifuging at 2000 rpm for 25 minutes with DI water and ethanol several times after that resulting sample was then collected and kept in vacuum drying oven at 60ºC for 24 hours.

To synthesis the MoS_2/rGO hybrid appropriate weight percentage of Graphene oxide (GO) was added to the above mixture and same process was done. In this method production yield of these materials is high and we can easily scale up the production of MoS_2 and rGo-MoS_2 hybrid materials by changing the amount of precursor in appropriate ratio.

7.2.2. MoS$_2$ and MoS$_2$/rGO thin film Preparation

To prepare thin film of MoS$_2$ and MoS$_2$/rGO hybrid, we have exfoliated as-prepared hydrothermal products in NMP followed by vacuum filtration on the cellulose membrane. After that the films were transferred on the Au-coated PET for further use as a working electrode. Careful measurement of film weight gives the area density of 23.23 μg /cm^2 for MoS$_2$/rGO hybrid film and 6.97μg/cm^2 for MoS$_2$ film.

7.3. Characterization:

Crystallinity and phase of the synthesized MoS$_2$ were characterized by X-ray diffraction, using Cu-Ka radiation (λ=1.541 A^0) on a D8 Advanced Bruker diffractometer. Surface morphology of prepared MoS$_2$ and MoS$_2$/rGO hybrid was investigated using FESEM, HITACHI S-4800.The morphology of the as prepared MoS$_2$ also analyzed by atomic force microscopy (AFM), Transmission electron microscopy (TEM) images were taken using JEOL-2010 transmission electron microscope instrument.

All electrochemical studies were carried out in a three electrode cell system using MoS$_2$ and hybrid film as a working electrode, platinum wire as a counter electrode, and an Ag/AgCl as a reference electrode with 1M H$_2$SO$_4$ aqueous solution as the electrolyte. All the electrochemical analysis including cyclic voltammetry (CV), galvanometric charging–discharging (CD), was carried out on CHI 660E electrochemical workstation.

7.4. Result & Discussion

7.4.1. Structural & morphological analysis:

An XRD pattern of the hydrothermally prepared MoS$_2$ is represented in the fig.7.1. All the diffraction peaks at 2θ value of 14.32° (002), 33.42 ° (100), 39.37 ° (103), 58.89 ° (110) in this pattern can be well-indexed to the hexagonal phase of MoS$_2$ (JCPDS card: 37-1492). The sharp peaks also indicate that the synthesized MoS$_2$ is well crystallized. The most intense peak at 2θ=14.32° (002) provides the interplanar spacing between the nanosheets (6.18A°), which indicates the formation of well-stacked layered structure of the MoS$_2$ nanosheets. Other d values corresponding to 2θ equal to 33.42°, 39.37°, and 58.89 ° are 2.67A°, 2.28A°, and 1.57A° respectively.

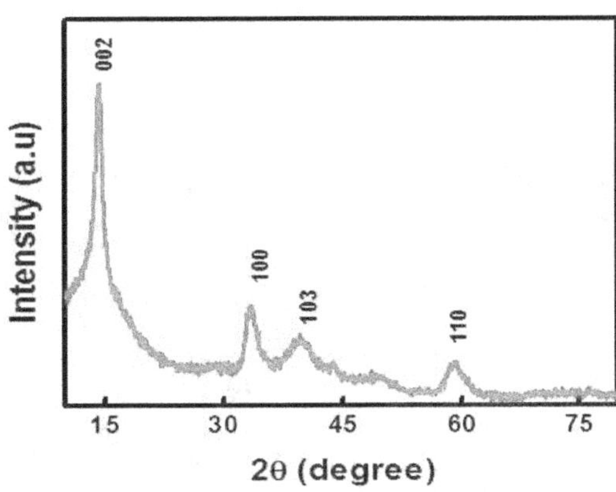

Figure 7.1. X-ray diffraction patterns of MoS_2.

Transmission electron microscope (TEM) image of the MoS_2 is taken on a holy carbon coated grid as shown in the figure 7.2(a)which shows sheet like structure of MoS_2 with lateral dimension of <500 nm long. Atomic force microscope image of the MoS_2 shown in the figure 7.2(b), indicates the thickness of MoS_2 nanosheets is 1.09 nm. TEM and AFM samples were prepared after bath sonication of MoS_2 in NMP.

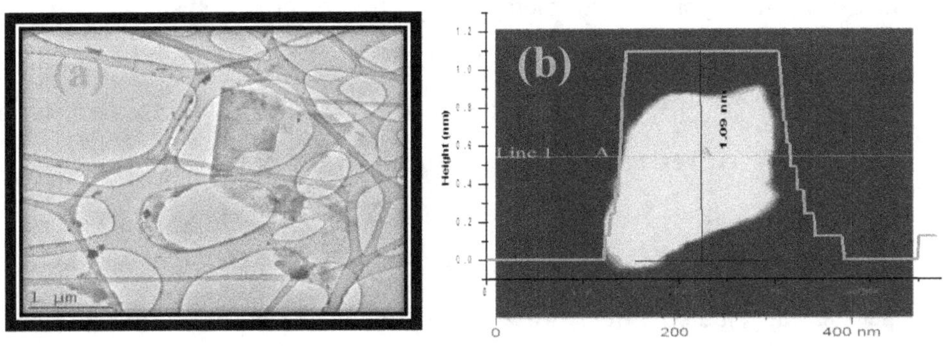

Figure. 7.2. TEM image of MoS_2, and (d) AFM image of MoS_2 nanosheets.

Figure 7.3(a) and 7.3(b) shows the FESEM images of MoS_2 and MoS_2/rGO hybrid respectively. FESEM image of bare MoS_2 figure 7.3(a) shows the Graphene like morphology, whereas the inset of figure 7.3(b) shows the presence of rGO clearly in the hybrid sample.

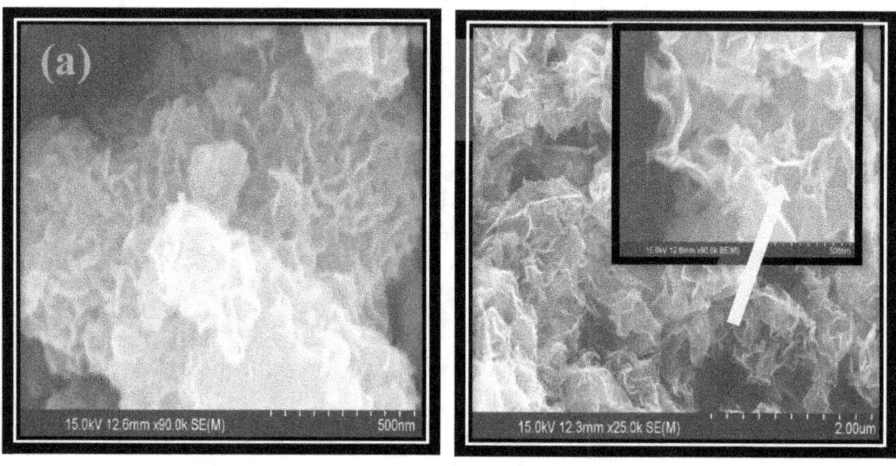

Figure.7.3. (a) FESEM images of MoS_2, (b) MoS_2/rGO.

7.4.2. Electrochemical Study:

The electrochemical performance of the electrode materials have been investigated measuring the cyclic voltammetry using three electrode system at different scan rates from 5 mV/s to100 mV/s with 1M H_2SO_4 aqueous solution as the electrolyte as shown in the figure 7.4(a). The areal capacitances of the hybrid electrode materials calculated from the CV curves to be 14.09mF/cm^2, 8.73 mF/cm^2, 4.025 mF/cm^2, 2.373mF/cm^2, and 1.493mF/cm^2 at 5, 10, 25, 50 and 100 mV/sec scan rates respectively. However the value of areal capacitance for MoS_2 electrode at 5 mV/s scan rate is 0.79mF/cm^2.The specific capacitance values are also calculated for both hybrid and MoS_2 electrodes. The corresponding obtained specific capacitance values are 607 F/g, 376 F/g, 173 F/g, 102 F/g, and 64 F/g at scan rates 5 mV/s, 10mV/s, 20mV/s, 50mV/s, 100mV/s respectively, whereas the specific capacitance value for the MoS_2 electrode is 113 F/g at 5mV/s. Firmiano, et al. [13] reported specific capacitance value of medium concentration MoS_2 and rGO was 265 F/g at 10 mV/sec scan rate whereas specific capacitance value of our sample at the same scan rate is 376 F/g. This might be due to high degree of exfoliation of materials in NMP which gives well dispersed ultrathin nanosheets of MoS_2 and rGO. Figure7.4 (b) represents the CV graphs of MoS_2 and MoS_2/rGO hybrid electrode at 5 mV/s scan rate. Changes of areal capacitance value of the hybrid electrode material with scan rate are shown in the figure 7.4(c). A plot of areal capacitance vs cycle numbers is shown in the figure 7.4(d), which shows almost 95% retention in the areal capacitance value over 1000 cycles.

Galvanostatic charge–discharge was also investigated at 0.02mA/cm^2 current density in the voltage range between 0 and 0.6 V for the both MoS$_2$ and MoS$_2$/rGO hybrid as shown in figure 7.5(a).The areal capacitance values obtained from GCD are 0.170mF/cm^2 and 11.75mF/cm^2 respectively. The hybrid material exhibits a high energy density of 5.71 mWh/cm^2 and a power density of 54.1 mW/cm^2.

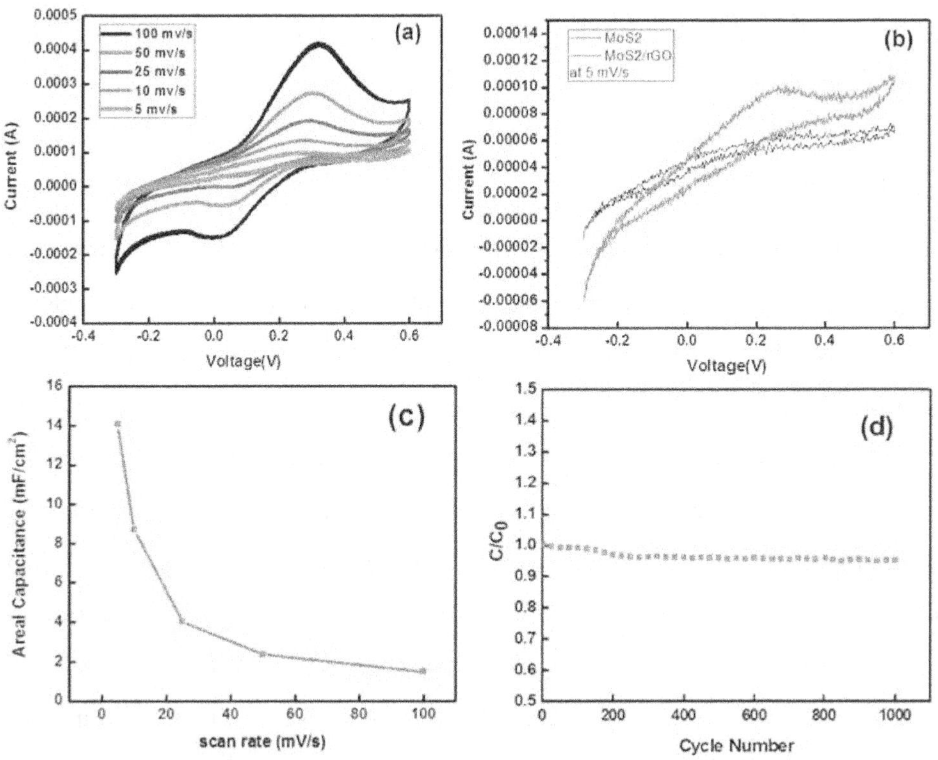

Figure.7.4. (a) CV graph of Hybrid materials at different scan rates,(b) CV graph of Hybrid materials and MoS$_2$ at 5 mV/s scan rate,(c)Areal capacitance vs scan rate graph of Hybrid material,(d) areal capacitance vs cycle number graph of hybrid material at 100mV/s.

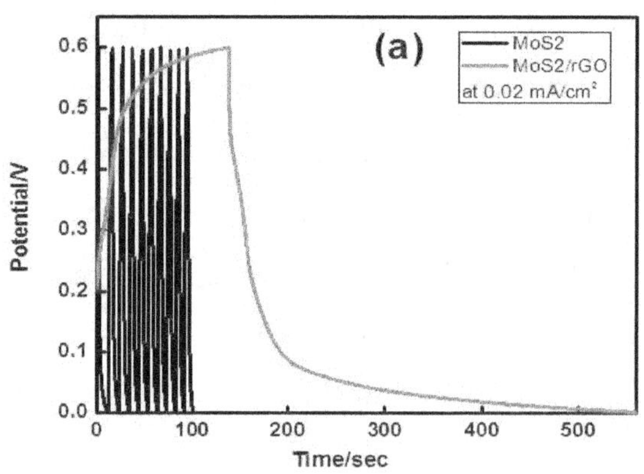

Figure.7. **5.** GCD graph of MoS_2 and MoS_2/rGO at constant current density at 0.02mA/cm^3

7.5.Summary

In summary, we have successfully synthesized MoS_2 nano sheets and MoS_2/rGO hybrid by hydrothermal route. Further, we have prepared thin film of hybrid electrodes on an Au coated PET to study the electrochemical nature of MoS_2 nanosheets and hybrid nanostructures of 2D - MoS_2/rGO nanosheets. The specific capacitance of hybrid electrodes was up to 14.09mF/cm^2 at 5mV/s, much higher than that of only MoS_2 electrodes 0.79mF/cm^2 at the same scan rate. Hybrid electrode exhibits high energy density of 5.71mWh/cm^2 and a power density of 54.1mW/cm^2. The composite electrode exhibits an excellent stability after 1000 cycles; almost 95% retention in the areal capacitance value over 250 cycles was seen for hybrid type electrode.Therefore MoS_2/rGO hybrids is a good choice as an electrode for supercapacitor application.

7.6. References

1) X. Yang, C. Cheng, Y. Wang, L. Qiu and D. Li, *Science*, 2013, 341, 534-537.

2) Y. Tao, et al. *Sci. Rep.*, 2013, **3**, 2975.

3) B. Radisavljevic , M. B. Whitwick , A. Kis , ACS Nano, 2011, **5**, 9934-9938.

4) S.Bertolazzi , J. Brivio , A. Kis , *ACS Nano*, 2011, **5**, 9703- 9709.

5) B. Radisavljevic , A. Radenovic , J. Brivio , V. Giacometti , A. Kis , *Nat. Nanotechnol.*, 2011, **6**, 147–150.

6) D. J. Late , B. Liu , H. S. S. R. Matte , V. P. Dravid and C. N. R. Rao , *ACS Nano*, , 2012, **6**, 5635–5641.

7) L. Mai, et al.*Sci. Rep.*, 2013, **3**, 1718.

8) B. E. Conway, *J. Electrochem. Soc.*, 1991, **138**, 1539.

9) P. Poizot, S. Laruelle, S. Grugeon, L.Dupont and J.M. Tarascon, *Nature*, 2000, **407**, 496–499.

10) E.Yoo, et al. *Nano Lett.* , 2008, **8**, 2277–2282.

11) P. Simon and Y. Gogotsi, *Nature Mater.*, 2008, **7**, 845-854.

12) M. Ghidiu,, M. R. Lukatskaya, MQ. Zhao, Y.Gogotsi and M. W.Barsoum, *Nature com.,* 2014, **516**, 78-81.

13) E. G. Da Silveira Firmiano, et al. *Adv. Energy Mater*, 2014, **4**, 1301380.

14) K.J Huang,. et al. *Electrochim. Acta*, 2013, **109**, 587–594.

Vanadyl Phosphate Nano sheets-MWCNT Composite Free standing thin film For Supercapacitor Application

Work presented in this chapter has been published in:

AIP Conf. Proc., 2016, 1728, 020479

Shibsankar Dutta, Sukanta De.

8.1. Introduction

It have been already seen that 2-dimensional nano materials are the suitable choice for the supercapacitor application due to their large specific surface area, electrochemical active sites, micromechanical flexibility, expedite ion migration channel properties. This chapter enlightens free standing hybrid films of functionalized MWCNT (–COOH group) and α-Vanadyl phosphates (VOPO$_4$ 2H$_2$O), prepared by vacuum filtering.

The performance of supercapacitor directly depends on the electrode materials. Therefore to improve the electrochemical performance of supercapacitor we need to develop new electrode materials with high capacitance behavior relative to the existing electrode materials for supercapacitor in the market. Till now active carbon material like carbon aerogels, Carbon nanotubes, reduced grapheme oxide etc. are widely used electrode materials due to the porous texture, high electrical conductivity, high specific surface area, good mechanical and thermal stability[3]. However the carbon based electrode materials have some limitation like high cost, low energy storage mechanism[4].To enhance the performance of supercapacitors inorganic metal oxides, sulphides, conducting polymers, transition metal phosphate were introduced as an electrode material, and the hybrid electrode materials enhanced the electrochemical performance due to the balanced of high specific surface area and high electrical conductivity[5]. S.L. Chou and co-workers has developed a novel electrode material MnO$_2$ nanowires over CNT paper, obtained the specific capacitance 167.5 F/ g at 77 mA/ g [6]. X. Lu et al. already reported CNT @V$_2$O$_5$ nano wire composite electrode materials resulting high specific capacitance 57.3 F/ g[7]. J. Ge and co-workers reported SWNT film on PET substrate as an electrode material, resulting specific capacitance 55.0 F/g at 2.6 A/ g[8]. Among these electrode materials (MnO$_2$,V$_2$O$_5$, MoS$_2$, MoO$_3$, RuO$_2$,VOPO$_4$ etc.) RuO$_2$ electrode obtained highest specific capacitance, but due to high cost, low abundance, high toxicity we need alternative electrode materials which also perform like RuO$_2$ electrode material.

Among all of the alternative candidates for supercapacitor transition metal phosphates like vanadyl phosphate dihydrate (VOPO$_4$, 2H$_2$O) have attained the attention due to high voltage upto 3.5 V, low cost and most importantly due to their environmental friendliness. Vanadyl phosphate dihydrate offered high potential compared to the oxides due to the peculiar layered structure in which V-O-P layers forms due to the corner sharing oxygen atom of PO_4 tetrahedral and VO_6 octahedral.[8,9] However, the conductivity of $VOPO_4.2H_2O$ is small compared to the other metal oxides and it plays a major drawback to the practical application.[9,10]Overcoming these limitations, we introduce a novel electrode material hybrid of $VOPO_4$ nanosheets and MWCNT in the present work.$VOPO_4$ nanosheets enhanced the electrochemical behavior because of their large specific surface area, high micromechanical flexibility, extra electrochemical active sites and MWCNT enhanced the electrical conductivity of the electrode materials.

8.2 Experimental

8.2.1. Synthesis of bulk vanadyl phosphate dehydrate

Bulk vanadyl phosphate dihydrate ($VOPO_4$·$2H_2O$) was prepared according to the previously reported literature[10]. 12gm V_2O_5 was added to the mixture of 68 ml H_3PO_4 and 290 ml DI water and refluxed at 110^0C for 16 h. Finally the yellow precipitate was collected by vacuumed filtration and thereafter the resulting sample was washed by DI water and Acetone several times and dried in vacuum at 60^0C.

8.2.2. Exfoliation of bulk $VOPO_4$·$2H_2O$

Bulk vanadyl phosphate dihydrate was dispersed into 2 propanol with an initial concentration 1mg/ml[10]. Thereafter the dispersion was ultrasonicated by bath sonication for 15 minutes to get vanadyl phosphate nanosheets, the resulting well dispersed nanosheets were used to make composite films.

8.2.3. MWCNT@$VOPO_4$·$2H_2O$ hybrid film

Initially commercially available MWCNT was dispersed into 2 propanol with bath sonication as previously reported literature.[11] Further, the dispersed solutions of MWCNT and $VOPO_4$·$2H_2O$ were added together and sonicated for couple of minutes to get well dispersed mixture of both. MWCNT-Vanadyl phosphate hybrid films were prepared by filtering an appropriate amount of mixed dispersion through polyvinylidene fluoride (PVDF) filtration membrane (Millipore, Durapore membrane filters, and 100 nm pore size). The deposited hybrid films were dried overnight under vacuum at 50^0C. Films were peeled off the filter membrane to get free standing hybrid films for detailed characterization.

8.3. Characterization

X-ray diffraction (XRD) analysis of powder sample was performed using a X-RAY DIFFRACTOMETER (XRD) Bruker D8. Raman spectra were recorded at room temperature with a Confocal Raman Microscope.Surface morphology was investigated with field emission scanning electron microscope (FESEM, HITACHI S-4800). The TEM images were taken on a JEOL-2010 transmission electron microscope instrument using an acceleration voltage of 200 kV. Cyclic voltammetry (CV) and galvanostatic charge–discharge tests were performed using an electrochemical analyzer (CHI660E) with two electrode cell using 1 M Na_2SO_4 as electrolyte.

8.4. Results and discussion

8.4.1. Structural & morphological analysis:

We have done powder X-ray diffraction (XRD) and Raman study to characterize as prepared $VOPO_4\cdot2H_2O$. As shown in Fig.8.1(a), the X-ray diffraction pattern of as prepared vanadyl phosphate dihydrate shows a set of diffraction peaks at $2\theta= 12.3^0$, $24.9^0$and 28.7^0 corresponding to (001),(002) and (102) planes with d values 0.71nm,0.36 nm,0.32 nm respectively. The formation of α phase of $VOPO_4\cdot2H_2O$ have confirmed from the XRD (JCPDS card No.84-0111) pattern.

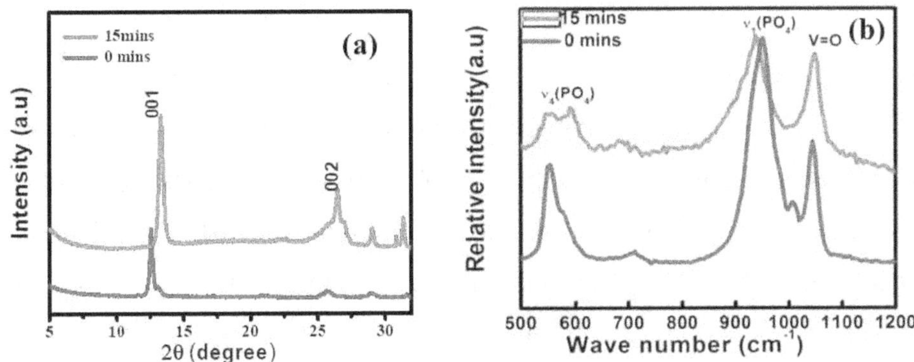

Figure8.1. (a) Powder XRD pattern and (b) Raman spectra of as prepared and exfoliated $VOPO_4\cdot2H_2O$

The relatively stronger (001) peak after exfoliation conforms formation of 2D $VOPO_4$ nanosheets. Moreover, shift of the (001) peak from lower 2θ (12.51°) to a higher (13.28°) during exfoliation, indicating the reduction of the interlayer spacing between two $VOPO_4$ layers, because of escape of H_2O molecules from interlayers.

The band at 950 cm^{-1} in the Raman spectrum (Fig.8.1b) for as prepared VOPO$_4$·2H$_2$O is corresponds to symmetric stretching vibration $v_1(PO_4)^{12}$ which shifted to lower wave number at 937 cm^{-1} for exfoliated VOPO$_4$. This shift is due to breaking of hydrogen bonds from oxygen atoms of the P-O bond in VOPO$_4$. The bands due to symmetric bending vibrations $v_4(PO_4)$ at 550 and 580 cm^{-1} also present in Raman spectrum for both as prepared and exfoliated vanadyl phosphate. The band at 1050 cm^{-1} is corresponding to V=O stretching mode. The Raman spectra confirmed that there is no obvious change in in–plane structure of VOPO$_4$.

Transmission electron microscopy (TEM) image of the exfoliated VOPO$_4$ nanosheets were taken on lacy carbon coated copper grid. Thin sheet like structures of VOPO$_4$ was observed under TEM (Fig.8.2a). Figure 8.2(b) shows the EDX pattern of VOPO$_4$ in which intense peaks observed corresponding to elements V, P and O.

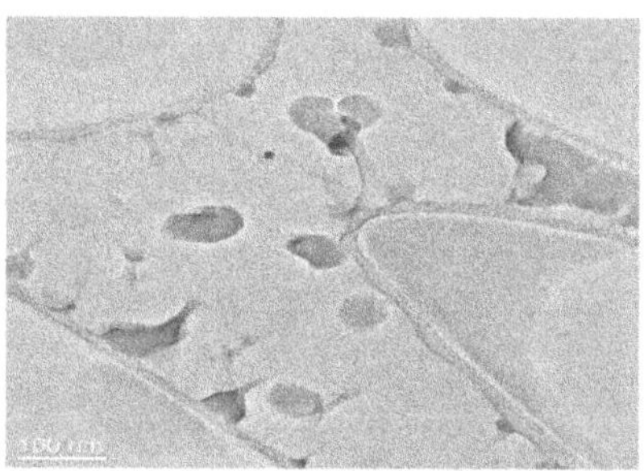
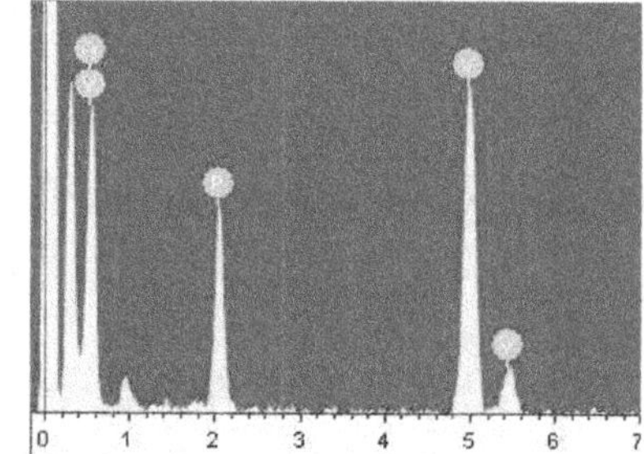

Figure 8.2. Low magnification TEM image (a) and EDX spectra (b) of VOPO$_4$ nanosheet

Scanning electron microscopy (SEM) was used to study the morphology of exfoliated VOPO$_4$ and the composite films. Shown in Figure 8.3(a) is a SEM image of exfoliated VOPO$_4$ which shows graphene like morphology of VOPO$_4$ after 15 mints sonication in 2 propanol. Figure 8.3(b) shows the FESEM image of MWCNT-VOPO$_4$ composite. This clearly shows the excellent mixing of VOPO$_4$ nanosheets into the MWCNT network and is uniformly distributed.

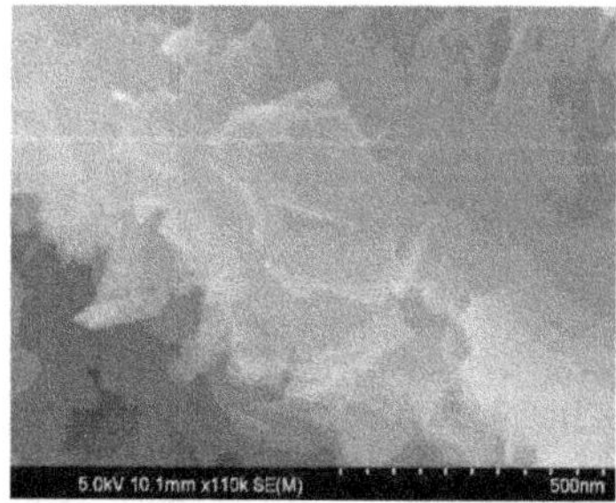
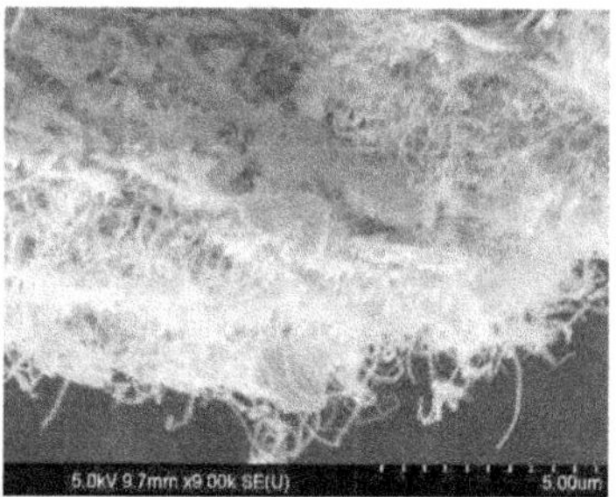

Figure 8.3.FESEM images of VOPO$_4$ nanoshees (a), VOPO$_4$/MWCNT (b)

8.4.2. Electrochemical Study:

To evaluate the performance of MWCNT-VOPO$_4$ hybrid films as electrode of supercapacitor, we have performed cyclic voltammetry (CV), galvanostatic charge-discharge (CD), and electrochemical impedance spectroscopy (EIS) tests using a two-electrode system. Figure 8.4(a) shows the CV curves of hybrid electrodes at different scan rates 5mV/s to 100 mV/s with a voltage window (-2.4 V to +2.4V). Redox peaks are observed in CV curve at about (+/-) 1V. CV measurements of pure MWCNT electrode are also tested which reveals the performance of hybrid electrode over the pure MWCNT electrode (Fig.8.4b). The charge storage mechanism of the electrode can be shown by the following reversible equation[13]

$$VO^{3+} + e^- + H^+ = HVO^{3+}$$

The specific capacitance values calculated from the CV curves to be 236, 179, 87, and 59 F/g at 5, 10, 50, and 100 mV/sec scan rates respectively for hybrid materials. However the value of specific capacitance for pure MWCNT electrode at 5 mV/sec scan rate is 49 F/g. From the charging discharging curves(Fig 8.4c) and (Fig 8.4d) the value of specific capacitance of pure MWCNT electrodes and hybrid electrodes were found to be 3F/g and 82 F/g at current density 1 A/g respectively. Specific capacitance calculated from CV curve for hybrid film is almost five times higher than that of MWCNT only film.

Further to evaluate the energy efficiency of supercapacitor based on hybrid materials of MWCNT-VOPO$_4$, energy density (E) and power density (P) were calculated from the CD curves in figure 4, using the equations $E = \frac{1}{2}CV^2$ and $P = \frac{E}{\Delta t}$, where C is the specific capacitance, V is the working voltage and Δt is the discharging time. Here we use the capacitance values calculated from CD curve. The supercapacitor based on hybrid materials deliver a high energy density of 65.6 Wh/Kg at a power density 1476 W/Kg which is superior to previously reported hybrid materials consist of 2D nanomaterials and carbon nanostructure[14,15]. From SEM image of hybrid film (Figure 8.3C), we have observed the excellent mixing of VOPO4 nanosheets into the MWCNT network and uniform distribution which should facilitate charge transport throughout the electrode and also mesoporous structure of hybrid allow access of electrolyte to the internal surface. This could be one reason of superior performance of supercapacitor based on MWCNT-VOPO$_4$ hybrid.

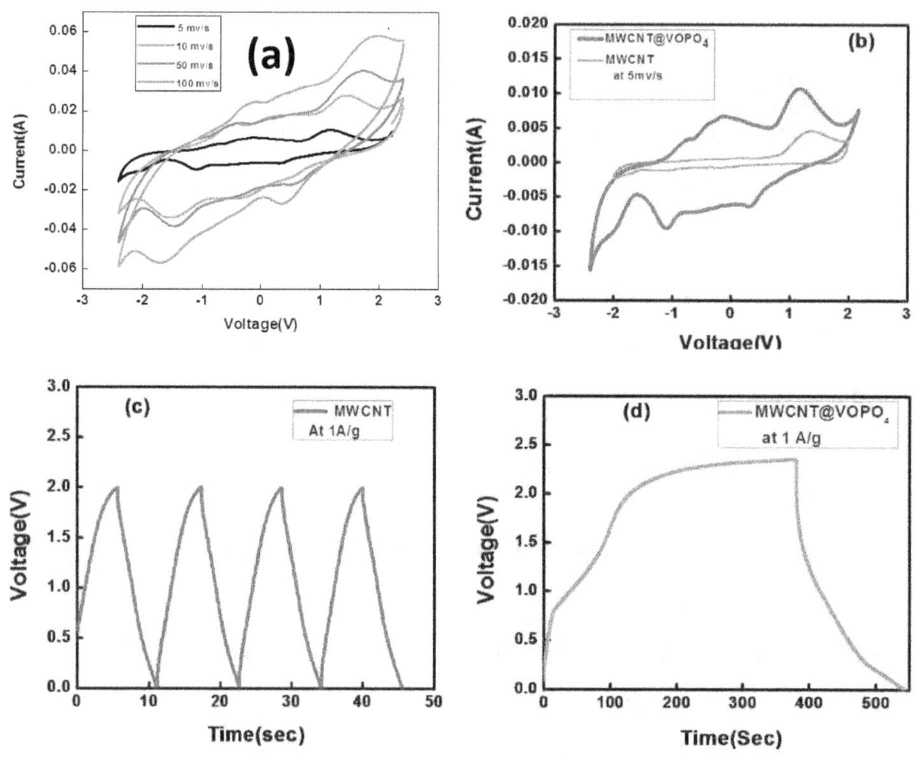

Figure 8.4. CV curves of hybrid electrodes at different scan rates (a), CV curves of MWCNT and hybrid electrodes at 5 mV/s(b),charging discharging curves of pure MWCNT(c) and hybrid electrodes(d) at 1 A/g

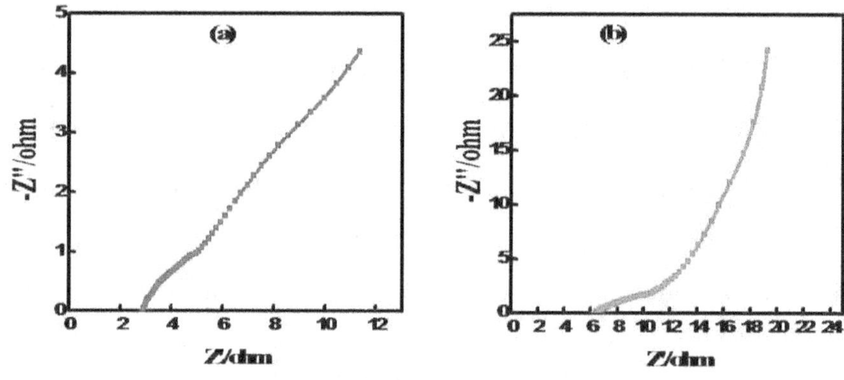

Figure 8.5. EIS plot of MWCNT electrodes (a), Hybrid electrodes (b)

We performed electrochemical impedance spectroscopy tests to evaluate the capacitive behavior of the supercapacitors. Fig. 8.5(a) and 8.5(b) shows Nyquist plots of MWCNT electrodes and hybrid electrodes respectively, where the ESR (equivalent series

119

resistance) for MWCNT electrodes and hybrid electrodes to be 2.9 ohm and 6 ohm respectively. The increase in series resistance of hybrid compare to only MWCNT film is obvious due to incorporation of $VOPO_4$. Higher the slope of the straight line at low frequency region in Nyquist plot implies better capacitive behavior of the devices. Here we can see from the figure 8.5(b) for hybrid film, the straight line at low frequency region in Nyquist plot is almost parallel to the imaginary axis, which indicates the ideal capacitive behavior of the supercapacitor based on MWCNT-$VOPO_4$ hybrid.

8.5 Summary

In summary, we have successfully synthesized vanadyl phosphate nano sheets in the simple exfoliation process. Further, to improve the electrochemical behavior MWCNT@$VOPO_4$ hybrid electrodes are prepared by vacuum filtering. The specific capacitance of hybrid electrodes was up to the 236 F/g at the scan rate 5 mV/s much higher than that of pure MWCNT electrodes (49 F/g) at the same scan rate. This MWCNT@$VOPO_4$ hybrid could be a good candidate for electrode of supercapacitor with superior energy efficiency.

8.6 .References

1. Xu Peng, Lele Peng, Changzheng Wu and Yi Xie, *Chem. Soc. Rev.,* 2014, **43**, 3303-3323.

2. H. Wang, H. S. Casalongue, Y. Liang and H. Dai, *J. Am.Chem. Soc.,* 2010, **132**, 7472–7477.

3. H. Shen, E.Liu, X.Xiang, Z.Huang, Y. Tian, Y.Wu, Z.Wu, H.Xie, *Mater.Res.Bull.,* 2012, **47**, 662-666.

4. A. Prakash, D. Bahadur, *ACS App. Mater. Inter.,* 2014, **6**, 1394-1405.

5. G. Wang, L. Zhang, J. Zhang, *Chem. Soc. Rev.* ,2012,**41**, 797-828.

6. S.L. Chou, J.Z. Wang, S.Y. Chew, H.K. Liu and S.X. Dou, *Electrochem. Commun.,* 2008, **10**, 1724–1727.

7. X. Lu, T. Zhai, X. Zhang, Y. Shen, L. Yuan, B. Hu, L. Gong, J. Chen, Y. Gao, J. Zhou, Y. Tong and Z. L. Wang, *Adv. Mater.,* 2012, **24**, 938–944.

8. J. Ge, G. Cheng and L. Chen, *Nanoscale,* 2011, **3**, 3084–3088.

9. Y. Sun, C. Wu, Y. Xie , *J Nanopart Res ,* 2010, **12**, 417–427.

10. C. Wu, X. Lu, L. Peng, K. Xu, X. Peng, J. Huang, G. Yu and Y. Xie, *Nat. Commun.,* 2013, **4**, 3431.

11. D.Hanlon, C.Backes, T.M.Higgins, M.Hughes, A.O'Neill, P.King, N.McEvoy, G.S.Duesberg, B.M.Sanchez, H.Pettersson, V. Nicolosi, and J. N. Coleman, *Chem. Mater.*,2014, **26**,1751-1763.

12. L.Benes, K. Melanova, M. Trchova, P. Capkova, and P.Matejka, *Eur. J. Inorg. Chem.*, 1999, 2289-2294.

13. Z.Luo, E. Liu, T.Hu, Z.Li, T. Liu, *Ionics*, 2015, **21**,289-294.

14. G. Yu, L.Hu, M. Vosgueritchian, H. Wang, X. Xie, J. R. McDonough, X. Cui, Y. Cui, and Z. Bao, *Nano Lett.* ,2011, **11**, 2905-2911.

15. L. Peng, X. Peng, B. Liu, C. Wu, Y. Xie, and G. Yu, *Nano Lett.*, 2013, **13**, 2151-2157.

Chapter 9

Conclusions and future works

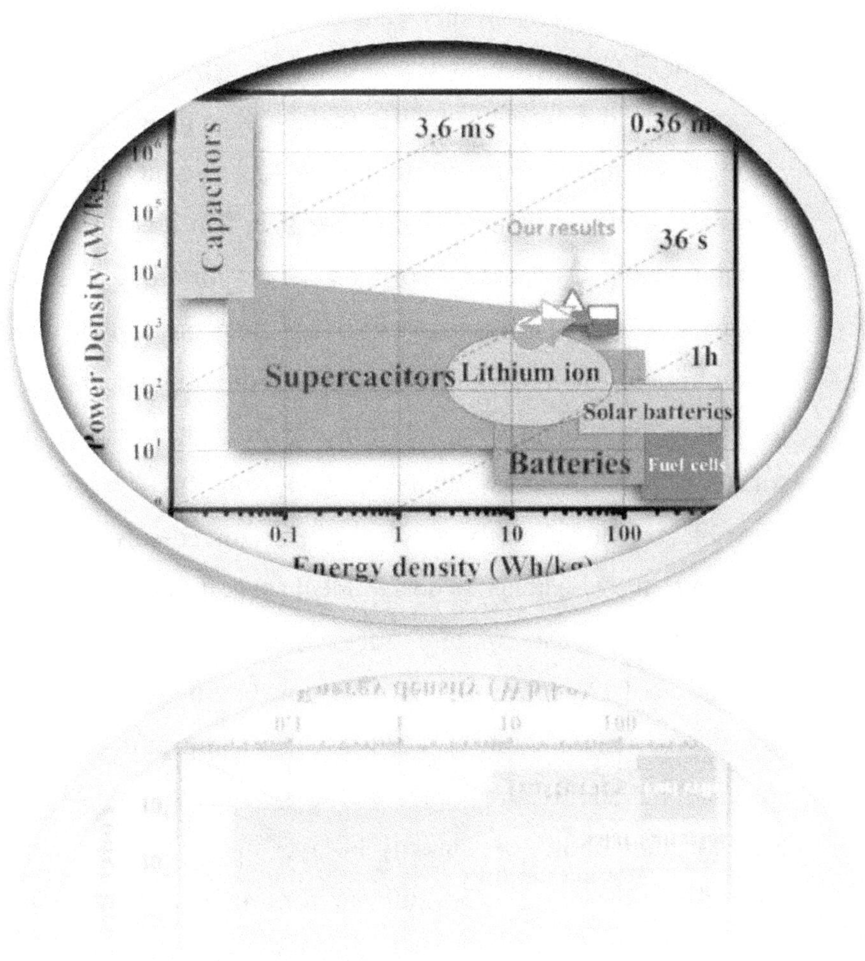

9.1 Conclusions of the thesis

The research work done in this thesis focused on the synthesis of 2-D nanomaterials and their nanocomposites for supercapacitor energy storage applications. For the development of supercapacitor, correct choice of electrode materials and electrolyte solutions are played very significant role. The following points emerged as conclusions from the detail works done described in the chapters 4-8 of the thesis:

1. A systematic study was done to prepare the 2-D nanosheets of TMOs from their bulks by mixed solvent exfoliation using ethanol and water. The results concludes two poor solvents ethanol and water can be a good solvent for exfoliating TMOs when they combined in a particular volume fraction. The versatile mixed solvent method is scalable and gives high concentration (0.42 mg/ml, 0.47 mg/ml and 0.40 mg/ml for MoO_3, MnO_2 and RuO_2 respectively) dispersion of TMOs nanosheets, higher than that reported previously. We have quantitatively analyzed the absorption spectra for all dispersions to optimize the volume fractions of water and ethanol to disperse TMOs. The results showed concentrations of TMOs dispersions are directly dependent on the volume fraction of ethanol in water with maximum concentration at 65% ethanol in water for MoO_3. Whereas for both MnO_2 and RuO_2 maximum concentration was obtained at 50% mixed solvent. This mixed-solvent strategy gives great freedom to the researches to design ideal solvent system from unlimited number of possible solvent mixture for various layered materials to exfoliate. Exfoliation of TMOs in mixture of two low boiling point solvents offers obvious advantages, including low cost, less toxicity compare to previously used organic solvents, no additive required, and easy removal. AFM and HRTEM and FESEM study shows that mostly bi-layer nanosheets are with average lateral size of 300 nm for MoO_3, 200 nm for MnO_2 and 100 nm for RuO_2 were obtained. The exfoliated nanosheets obtained specific surface area of 55.7 m^2/g, 48.6 m^2/g, 53.5 m^2/ g for MoO_3, MnO_2 and RuO_2 nanosheets respectively. Whereas, the total specific surface area of 151.4 m^2/g, 122.8 m^2/g, 142.6 m^2/g were obtained for the MoO_3/SWCNT, MnO_2/SWCNT and RuO_2/SWCNT nanocomposites respectively. The large specific surface area and mesoporous structure provides more active sites and shortening ion diffusion paths between electrode and electrolyte for electrochemical reactions, which reflected in the electrochemical result obtained for SWCNT/TMOs thin films supercapacitor.

The MoO_3/SWCNT flexible symmetric solid state supercapacitor delivered maximum specific capacitance of 717 F/g at 5 mV/s, whereas MnO_2-SWCNT and RuO_2-SWCNT symmetric supercapacitor exhibited a   specific capacitance of 540 F/g and 676 F/g respectively. The symmetric supercapacitors exhibit excellent flexibility and long cycle life, leading to an extremely high energy density (24.89 Wh/Kg at 1.61 kW/kg, 18.73 Wh/Kg at 1.21 kW/Kg and 23.48 Wh/Kg at 1.52 kW/Kg), whereas, in-plane micro supercapacitors based on few layered MnO_2 and SWCNT hybrid displayed excellent specific capacitance of 560.22 F/g with significant energy density of 77.80 Wh/kg.

2. A systematic study was conducted for the synthesis of $BiVO_4$ nanoparticle by varying the hydrothermal reaction conditions. The well crystalline $BiVO_4$ nanoparticles having almost same in shape and size with an average dimension of ~20–30 nm are obtained at the optimum growth duration of 90 min. The growth mechanism of the morphology was investigated by SEM analysis. We have also synthesized $BiVO_4$ embedded rGO hybrid nanostructure with three different GO concentrations by a simple cost effective hydrothermal method. Structure, surface morphology and capacitive behaviours of $BiVO_4$/rGO hybrid were well investigated. We have studied the electrochemical properties of as prepared hybrid to know its performance as symmetric supercapacitor electrodes with both PVA/H_2SO_4 solid and Na_2SO_4 aqueous electrolytes. The obtained maximum specific capacitance is 400 F/g at 5 mV/s scan rate in solid electrolyte and 245 F/g in aqueous Na_2SO_4 at same scan rate. High energy density (35.37 Wh/Kg) and excellent cycle stability makes this hybrid suitable for application in supercapacitor.

3. Well crystalline BiOCl nanoplates were prepared by simple hydrothermal route. BiOCl /MWCNT based nanocomposites with different weight percentage of BiOCl as electrodes were designed for light-weight flexible high performance thin film supercapacitor. As prepared nanoplates was characterized by XRD, Raman, FESEM, TEM and XPS. The N_2 adsorption–desorption measurement result shows among different compositions, composite with 60 wt% BiOCl exhibits maximum specific surface area of 22.750m^2/g . The 60 wt% BiOCl composite flexible supercapacitor delivered highest specific capacitance of 421F/g and energy density 14.62 Wh/Kg. Excellent cycle stability with only 6% reduction in specific capacitance after 2000 cycles and good stability under

bending, making the fabricated supercapacitor extremely promising as a flexible energy storage device.

4. MoS$_2$ nano sheets and MoS$_2$/rGO hybrid also synthesized by hydrothermal route. The thin film of hybrid electrodes on an Au coated PET obtained specific capacitance of of 14.09mF/cm^2 at 5mV/s, much higher than that of only MoS$_2$ electrodes 0.79mF/cm^2 at the same scan rate. Hybrid electrode exhibits high energy density of 5.71mWh/cm^2 and a power density of 54.1mW/cm^2. The composite electrode exhibits an excellent stability after 1000 cycles.

5. Vanadyl phosphate nano sheets/MWCNT free standing thin films were prepared by vacuum filtering. The nanocomposite electrode yielded a specific capacitance of 236 F/g at the scan rate 5 mV/s much higher than that of MWCNT electrodes (49 F/g) at the same scan rate. The nanocomposite electrode exhibited energy density of 65.6 Wh/Kg at a power density 1476 W/Kg. could be a good candidate for electrode of supercapacitor with superior energy efficiency.Fig. 9.1 represents the Ragone plot of our 2-D material based supercapacitor compare with reported literature. Overall, the work based on the 2-D nanomaterials presented in this thesis mostly enhanced the energy storage performance of the supercapacitors towards light weight flexible energy storage device applications.

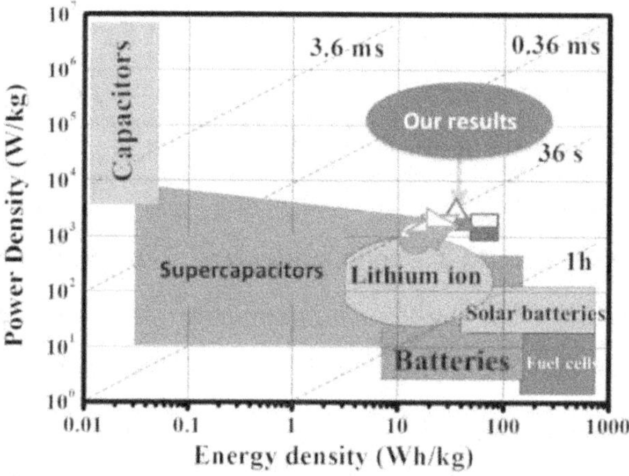

Figure 9.1. Ragone plot of our 2-D material based supercapacitor compare with reported literature.

9.2 Future Works

In recent years due to the fast development of electronic devices including flexible smart window, flexible transparent touch screens, electronic books etc., investigation on flexible transparent electrodes has attracted huge attention.[1–5] commercially available transparent ITO (Indium tin oxide) electrode may be replaced by carbon nanotubes (CNTs)[6], graphene[7], metal nanowires[8], Conductive polymers based transparent electrode to improve the performance of supercapacitor. Energy density is directly proportional to the square of the voltage window as well as the capacitance value, so enhancement of the energy density can be done by increasing both voltage window and capacitance value. Adding redox-active materials such as copper chloride, potassium iodide, hydroquinone etc. into the electrolytes is an easy process to improve the electrochemical performances because of extra pseudo capacitance contribution from the redox active electrolyte at the electrode-electrolyte interface.

Some of the future prospects of these present research works can be explored as follows

1. BiOCl/SWCNT based flexible transparent high performance supercapacitors.
2. Fe_2O_3/SWCNT based flexible transparent thin film supercapacitor with AgNWs as current collector.
3. Improve electrochemical performance of BiOCl/rGO supercapacitors after adding redox-active materials to the electrolyte.

9.3 References

1. S. De, P.E. Lyons, S. Sorel, E.M. Doherty, P.J. King, W.J. Blau, P.N. Nirmalraj, J.J. Boland, V. Scardaci, J. Joimel, J.N. Coleman, *ACS Nano* ,2009, **3**,714–720.
2. H.Z. Geng, K.K. Kim, K.P. So, Y.S. Lee, Y. Chang, Y.H. Lee, *J. Am. Chem. Soc.*,2007,**129**,7758–7759.
3. Y. Zhou, F. Zhang, K. Tvingstedt, S. Barrau, F. Li, W. Tian, O. Inganäs, *Appl. Phys. Lett.*,2008,**92**, 2006–2009.
4. G. Eda, Y.Y. Lin, S. Miller, C.W. Chen, W.F. Su, M. Chhowalla, *Appl. Phys. Lett.*, 2008, **92**,10–13.

5. W. Hong, Y. Xu, G. Lu, C. Li, G. Shi, *Electrochem. Commun.* ,2008, 101555–1558.

6. X. Wang, L. Zhi, K. Müllen, *Nano Lett.*, 2008, **8**,323–327.

7. S. Bae, H. Kim, Y. Lee, X. Xu, J.S. Park, Y. Zheng, J. Balakrishnan, T. Lei, H. Ri Kim, Y. Il Song, Y.J. Kim, K.S. Kim, B. Özyilmaz, J.H. Ahn, B.H. Hong, S. Iijima, *Nat. Nanotechnol.*,2010,**5**,574–578.

8. J. Lee, P. Lee, H.B. Lee, S. Hong, I. Lee, J. Yeo, S.S. Lee, T.S. Kim, D. Lee, S.H. Ko, *Adv. Funct. Mater.*,2013,**23**,4171–4176

9. N. Kim, S. Kee, S.H. Lee, B.H. Lee, Y.H. Kahng, Y.R. Jo, B.J. Kim, K. Lee, *Adv. Mater.*, 2014, **26**,2268–2272.